SPIRIT GARDENS

SPIRIT GARDENS

Rekindling Our Nature Connection

MINNIE S. KANSMAN

The mission of this book is to serve the readers with practical information that encourages personal gardening independence in harmony with the environment. Enabling gardeners to expand their view of their gardens to living adventures filled with glorious possibilities and life enriching outdoor rooms.

This publication is intended to provide educational information for the reader on the covered subject. None of the information is intended to take the place of personalized medical counseling, diagnosis and treatment from a trained health professional.

ISBN 978-0-9797681-1-8
Library of Congress Catalog Card Number: 2007904782
1. gardening 2. feng shui gardening 3. organic gardening 4. medicinal herbs
5. nature spirits 6. garden ritual

Edited by Roberta H. Binder
Cover design by Sue Conrad
Text design by Fiona Raven
Photograph credits see Acknowledgements
Graphics by Stephan Kansman

First Printing October 2007
Printed in India

Published by Devas Publishing Company
12325 36th Street SE, Lowell, MI 49331

DEVAS
Publishing

I dedicate this book to my Mom,
the Nature Lady,
June Hamilton.
She opened my eyes
to Nature's gifts
from the very start.

And also to the Nature Spirits themselves,
I appreciate the nudge.

Dicentra spectabilis 'Alba'

CONTENTS

Foxglove (Digitalis, spp.)
is a flower the fairies love
and are attracted to

WITH GRATITUDE ✢

A book starts out as an isolated seed of creativity, with the author holding the space for it to be. As it takes root and begins to grow, so many others contribute to building the final structure. I have had so many enthusiastic caregivers for this book; she has been in such good hands.

The first to hear of this idea and begin to nourish the soil were my family. My husband Rein has always been a strong, sturdy trellis for me to lean on and share ideas with. I thank him with all my heart. My children Stephan and Jessica, both who allowed me to share their personal experiences in this book, have always loved me as deeply as I have loved them. Thanks for understanding when my attention was elsewhere because of this project.

Then the book idea started to be shared with close and understanding friends. Marjorie Morrison, Paula Blumm, Julie Kienitz-Peak, Mimi Ray, and Denise Mason; you all saw and helped hold my vision from the start. And then the plant burst forth from the soil and saw the light of day.

Groups of people began to share in the development of every stem and leaf. *Book Study Group:* Cynthia Brant, Elaine Feldman, Meredyth Parrish Ph.D., Barbara Nash, Carol Ligda-Wong, Dawn Skinner, Beth Lively, Jan Bunker, Kelly Hagger. You all made such a difference in its growth and in my confidence to continue feeding it. Then came the *Interior Alignment Group*, especially the e-group, who encouraged me with their love and cheers of support so often. Thank you.

Others who have been monumental to the success of this endeavor are: Denise Linn, my Editor Roberta H. Binder, Ann Kuehn, Michelle Morrison, Carmen Hannah, Patti Heredia, Jeanette Cake, Mary Balkon, Sue Conrad, Tressa Mills, and Jay at Spirit Dreams. A big thank you goes to Fiona Raven, for holding my hand through the design and printing process, and adding her amazing creative style to the beauty of this book. I also want to thank my extended family of the Hamilton's and the Kansman's, who have taught me the big lessons of love and gratitude. May the love felt in this book continue to blossom in all of your hearts.

Love and Blessings, Minnie

FOREWORD ⬎

It was still dark as we piled into the van. Minnie slid into the passenger seat next to me, while other friends piled into the back of the van.

"I'm glad that you're riding shotgun today," I said.

"Hey, today's my birthday! I'm excited about our excursion."

"Well, hold on because it's going to be a bit of an adventure," I said.

We were all on a journey high into the Cascade Mountains to gather sage for use in sacred ceremonies. We left while it was still dark so that we would be high in the mountains for the sunrise. The road on which we traveled was rarely used and was perilous in places, so I drove slowly to avoid potholes and the treacherous steep edge.

As I drove, the first red light of the morning began to illuminate the western horizon. In the distance across the valley we could see the snow-clad Mt. Rainier, piercing the sky with its massive grandeur. I glanced at the petite woman sitting next to me. Her eyes sparkled. The sound of her voice was so musical, each word sounded almost like a tiny chime. As she spoke about her love of plants and of her love of nature, her vibrancy seemed to fill the entire van. I could sense that there was something remarkable about this woman.

At the top of a high plateau, I pulled the van up to the edge and stopped. In every direction the tops of mountain ranges were catching the first golden light of the sunrise.

"Not far from here is some sage growing in a mountain meadow." I pointed to a place not far away.

"Because you will be using this sage for sacred purposes, I suggest that you approach it using similar methods to those used by ancient and native cultures whenever they used plants for hallowed purposes. When you use these methods, the spirit of the plant won't die when it is picked, but in fact it will become much stronger."

"First, draw near the sage with reverence. Stand before it and imagine that you are breathing in the essence or the soul of the plant. Then reach out and hold one of the branches and *ask* the plant if it is all right to pick it. If you get the *feeling* that it is right, then go ahead and break or cut that branch, but never take an over abundance from one plant" I explained.

Slowly the women each walked off in search of sage. Through the pine trees I watched as Minnie approached a sage bush. There was a grace and dignity within her that engulfed the space around her as she walked. Butterflies – hundreds of them – flitted and tumbled through the plants near her. The connection that Minnie had told me she had with Nature was palpable. I watched as she approached a large gray-green sage bush and slowly kneeled before it, putting her hand out to lightly touch it. It was almost as if I could hear the sage sigh in the joy that it felt from that touch. I smiled in deep pleasure at witnessing that moment.

A couple of hours later Minnie walked toward me with small bundles of sage gathered in her arms. Her face was glowing. The sage was glowing. I knew that this was truly sacred sage for sacred purposes. As we climbed back into the van Minnie said, "This is the best birthday present that I have ever received!"

Hearing those words, my heart became full.

In this book Minnie will help you explore the magical realm of plants and gardens. With the same loving attention that she gave the sagebrush that morning, she will gently share with you how to create gardens of pleasure, love and healing.

Denise Linn
International Author of *Sacred Space*,
Feng Shui for the Soul, and many more.

INTRODUCTION ✒

This book is about my personal gardening experiences of working in tandem with the unseen Nature Spirits and energies found on my land. It is my desire to share an enlightening story or two, as well as some practical advice on how I connect with this divine kingdom everyday. May it inspire you to do the same in your garden space or while outside walking in Nature. I will also share my experiences using the ancient art of feng shui as I have applied it to my own garden spaces and those of clients. I encourage you to expand beyond the sometimes confining one-dimensional view of visual reality, to something much deeper and richer. Let the child in you remember how closely you once adored Nature, and relish again in the possibility of being a part of the magic that resides there.

I am concerned for our society when I see how disconnected from Nature we have become. On a typical day we might enter our car through the built-in garage, drive to work on paved roads, park in a concrete lot, enter the building through the parking garage, and work in a stuffy, sealed window, climate controlled space all day. Reversing this pattern at the end of the day and arriving back home to an air-conditioned house, we may have actually never touched the earth, or had any sensory stimulation from Nature all day!

How did we come, in a mere hundred years or so, from centuries of living in homes with dirt floors, soft and smooth beneath our feet to those with pristine white polyester carpeting above layers of floorboard and foam padding? When did the "soil of the earth" become a dirty word, and why? As we became more wealthy and refined, we separated further from the land. Shelter became more than a place to keep us safe from the elements, it became a protective bubble where we disconnected from Mother Nature.

In contrast, take a look at the indigenous tribes and their lifestyles. No one lives in closer connection to Nature, because they do literally live in closer proximity. The celebrations and rituals I describe in this book, many derived from such cultures, help to bring us back to our roots. They help to remind us of how much there is to receive from this planet we live on. I am not saying we all need to revert back to dirt floors and poverty to connect with our source. I suggest we notice how separated we have become in a relatively short period of time. Only two generations back, my grandfather and his entire family lived close to the rhythms of Nature because he was a farmer. They rose with the roosters and went to bed with the sun. They were not afraid of getting dirty; in fact, it was just a part of everyday life.

So this book is about getting dirty again, using gardening as Nature's lesson plan. A garden is the best teacher of the cycles of life and death. This book will give you the tools to see your garden as a way to connect back yourself, and the cycles you have always been a part of.

A kaleidoscope of color can be found hidden inside a simple red tulip

Spirit Gardens has been inside me since my childhood. I have always been a gardener in my Soul. I think it is in my DNA. I'm sure I chose my mother in this lifetime to be my teacher and mentor about all that is nature. After all, she was titled "The Nature Lady" at Girl Scout Camp when I was nine years old! Through her, my discovery of all things wild and mysterious began. She instilled in me a sense of awe, respect, and compassion for the green world.

Of course Mom is an avid gardener herself. My first memories of her are watching her bending over the flowers and actually talking to them. I can remember her coming home from teaching school in early spring and heading directly to the flower garden, purse and paperwork in hand. She was checking the progress of growth and also for any new arrivals that had poked their noses through the soil that day.

My intimate connection with flowers began early in life. One day as a very young child, I was in my mother's side garden looking for and smelling all the beautiful bulbs that had opened their faces on that first warm spring day. One brilliant red tulip caught my eye, and as I peeked inside, my heart was filled with awe. Inside I found an entire universe of intricate color and pattern. It was like looking into Nature's toy kaleidoscope for the first time! I remember checking the inside of every tulip after that to see what surprise each held for me.

Then one glorious summer Mom gave me a three by five foot garden plot all my own. I loved growing morning glories on the fence behind it from seed. The miracle of their rapid growth was amazing to a six-year-old. When they began to bloom I made a game of counting the grand total of sky-blue blossoms that opened every morning. I remember rushing out in my pajamas to a count of sixty-five one day. What a glorious sight!

I now find myself heading straight into my garden when I arrive home, just like Mom did. The flowers are always waiting for me, and judging from their growth I can imagine all that has occurred in my absence.

I have always had a garden. I always will.

DEAR NATURE SPIRITS

I know you exist as I can feel you and see you in my mind's eye. You have always been present in my life and I would like to introduce you to those who may not know you yet. Gardening is the perfect way to connect. Your energy becomes the thoughts and ideas that emerge in my mind as I work Zen-like in my garden. Or even as I look out the window on a snowy afternoon and dream of the garden work, which never feels like work, that is to come. I have plans, big plans and dreams that pop into my mind and you are there to help refine them and bring them into manifestation. All of it is to create beauty in my world and the world of those around me, to heal all of our needs and bring us closer to God, who in the end is responsible for it all. I feel so blessed to be a part of this plan to link the two together and often I hear pure joy rise inside my Soul as I answer that call. In gratitude for all I have and will learn from you on this planet, thank-you!

AMEN

CHAPTER I

RECONNECTING
WITH THE EARTH

◆

When we stop and take time to listen, to sense, and to just *be* with the energy of our surroundings, a shift occurs within us and we never see with the same eyes again. Many people who work with the earth through gardening, farming, or natural studies have already felt and are living with that shift. I think it is a remembering that we are an important part of the vast force in Nature that is all knowing and all giving. Call it God, call it Great Spirit, call it Love, but know it is out there and has never really left us. As my dear friend and wise woman Rachael Salley says, "When God and I are far apart, who moved?" May this book inspire you to reconnect or deepen your connection with the earth through the vehicle of gardening.

So together, at the beginning of this journey, let us discover ways to rekindle this connection. As I said before, paying attention to what is happening in your immediate environment is a great place to begin. When I was a child, I took it for granted that everyone talked to their plants, just like they talked to their dog or their cat. Yes, I know animals can't speak English and talk back, but that doesn't mean you can't have a conversation with them. They speak in others ways, through body language and through pictures in your mind. My

Bleeding heart (Dicentra spectabilis) is a heart connection flower

1

cat stands and waits at her water bowl, and I know she is thirsty and wants fresh water. The dog has a wistful glaze to her eyes; I can tell she is missing my husband who is away on a business trip.

Likewise, looking at a plant with drooping leaves, you know it wants a drink. A plant with dull or yellowing leaves needs some fertilizer, and a one with brown holes is getting too much sun. Once you know about plants, these messages are obvious. At times this communication is what I call a knowingness, a sixth sense about what is needed. For instance, seeing an extra glow or vitality emanating from a plant, I know it is happy in its location. Sensing a dull lifeless energy from a plant lets me know it needs my attention, and is often asking to be moved elsewhere in the garden.

Watching my mother talk to plants since my childhood has given me the advantage of never questioning this practice of communication. But as I grew older, I did begin to question just whom or what was she speaking to? Was it the physical structure of the plant, or was there something more? This is when I discovered Nature Spirits, or Devas, and also that other people talked to them too. In fact, entire books have been written about the Devas and the energy they bring to a garden. I know many people garden without ever tapping into this dimension, and still they enjoy the physical rewards gardening provides. Yet Nature Spirits add a layer of spiritual dimension to gardening that takes one beyond growing an award winning tomato, or creating an eye-catching flowerbed. This relationship takes us deeper into our sacred self, and richly feeds our Soul.

It is a pleasure knowing this gardening "secret": that there is another dimension that is overlapped with the one we can see with our physical eyes. I am so grateful that there is an entire group of entities in the garden just waiting for me to ask for their help! By working together, we can build a paradise of sacred space that is filled with light and becomes a haven for all who experience it.

I feel more than see this other dimension and it is translated into a sense of personal joy, love and healing when I am open to it. The palatable energy is everywhere in Nature, not just in a garden. It is even on a city sidewalk living within the one stubborn dandelion plant that refuses to surrender to such harsh conditions. It is in a remote tundra landscape, sleeping quietly under several feet of snow. Acknowledging that it exists is what began my relationship with it.

Keeping this open heart and mind has led me to question many more unknowns in my gardening life. I have discovered the energies found in a garden are not there by accident. There is a very organized and orchestrated plan to all that helps a garden to thrive. And the human factor is but one of many in this equation, the one factor the Nature Spirits have been waiting to reconnect with for a very long time.

GARDEN DEVAS

It was mid-June and just a few weeks after moving into a new home that I encountered my own Landscape Deva. I was eagerly raking new topsoil over the barren sand on the East side of the yard. My goal was to get the lawn seed planted by that weekend so I would perhaps have a green and glowing lawn sometime that summer. As I raked, a sense of a very tall angelic-like presence came swooping around the corner of the house, as if in anticipation. She was a wispy white color, much the texture of silk or gauze flowing in the wind. I could see her face clearly, but the rest of her body flowed into this white, transparent energy shape, seeming to float about two to three feet off the ground. I knew who she was without having to ask, and in our acknowledgement of each other I was shown the yard in the future tense.

As I looked at the new barren ground around me, I saw the lawn as green and lush, the perennial beds bursting with color and light. I could see clear as day the Children and Creativity Garden in its full splendor. There was a trickling fountain in one corner, and orange and yellow tiger lilies, purple coneflower, black-eyed susans, and old-fashioned delicate pink fairy roses filling up the space. To my left I saw the Helpful People Garden, with a 2-foot gray statue of a sitting Buddha surrounded by pink and white Japanese anemones. A golden ginkgo tree loomed over the Buddha's head providing a serene sense of shelter in the dappled shade. The Landscape Deva was pleased with my labors and my heart was buzzing with excitement. I smiled to her and myself, knowing this was truly going to be a magical experience for us both in the seasons ahead.

Three years after that meeting, I stand in the same spot on the Southeast side of the yard. I smile at the lush growth of emerald green grass beneath my feet. In the near distance a rotund statue of Buddha sits quietly under the protective branches of a delicate golden ginkgo tree. The bright pink petals of the japanese anemones sway in the breeze. My gaze moves down the hill to

The fairy gardens as seen with the Landscape Deva three years before it was planted

the Fairy Garden in the Children and Creativity area. It is ablaze with color. Fluorescent purple echinacea on sturdy stalks, brilliant yellow lilies, and vibrant black-eyed susans shine their cheery faces towards the sky. The sound of water trickling in the distance from the three-tiered fountain is comforting and cooling on this hot summer's day. I am now physically surrounded by the exact visual the Landscape Deva had given me years ago, when all this was only sand and rocks as I raked the dark brown topsoil over its surface. She had shown me the magic to come; I had seen the vision of the garden years before it was complete.

For me this type of visioning helps to manifest all the parts that eventually become a garden. When we can see it in our mind's eye complete, or are able to sketch a visual image on paper, the real work has already been accomplished. Learning how to communicate with your Landscape Deva will greatly assist you in this process.

Nature Spirits, also known as Nature Devas, are the unseen energies of a natural space that orchestrate all that occurs in that place. The three levels that most humans interact with when working in a garden are Landscape Devas, Plant and Animal Devas, and Fairies. Forming a relationship with them ensures an easier and more joyful process of gardening. It takes gardening to the deeper and more intimate level of working in co-creation with another dimension of life to enrich the harmony of the land we live on.

The most beautiful and accurate definition of Deva I have ever heard is: "*That which brings light.*" Is it any wonder that the words Deva and Angel are often used interchangeably? Devas take light and manifest it into the beautiful three-dimensional flowers, fruits, vegetables, and plants that grow in our gardens. Every garden, plot of land, and expanse of grass has a Landscape Deva connected with it. This Deva works like the general contractor for all that is growing in that space. It orchestrates the overall vitality found in that particular organized area of the garden.

As I have said, I have often seen this Landscape Deva in my mind's eye moving down a swoop of beautiful emerald green grass on a hill at the Southeast side of my garden, even when it was still all just bare sand. She moves like the energy I call Chi flow, the life force that is in all living things. Often I sense her as more of a feeling than an image, yet I do sometimes see a billowing, gauzy, haze and the color white. She loves racing around that corner to greet me and to fill my heart with pure glee. This Landscape Deva is beauty and grace and ease of motion. She is the essence of my garden in full bloom, as it sways in all its colors on a breezy afternoon. She emulates the feeling I wish to create in all places, everywhere; inside and outside my home. She is peaceful tranquility, and she is alive!

The plants in turn are governed by the energies of an Overlighting Deva for each plant family. For example, the Rose Deva is in charge of making sure that its plants create the awesome, sweet smelling flowers we recognize as roses. The Carrot Deva is in charge of the cellular and energetic makeup found in the plant that directs it to form carrots. There are also Devas in charge of species of animals, for instance the Mole Deva. This is the energy you would want to communicate with if you were having a maze of mole tunnels crisscrossing your garden. We will discuss more about that in the Natural Gardening chapter!

Each plant may also have its own individual Deva, and often these are called Fairies. Fairies help to form the physical structure of each particular plant within the family group. In my garden I have never seen a fairy in the form made popular in storybooks, the tiny humanlike creatures with gossamer wings, though I would love to. It is said fairies will appear to you in the form you feel most comfortable seeing them in. What I *perceive* as fairies are tiny golden dots surrounding a plant or as a light green to white wispy flow that comes in and out of my visual perception. I most often sense it when I am not looking for it; for instance when my physical body takes over the labor that needs to be done, like the digging or watering, and a rich humming feeling takes over my mind. These are the times when I get to sense my gardens' true energy; huge and all encompassing, yet sometimes it condenses so I get a glimpse of its wonder.

It wasn't until I studied feng shui and developed my ability to focus on Chi flow that I began to visually *see* the Nature Spirits. Working in the garden, a sense of present moment mindfulness comes over me and the rest of the world is far away. One day as I was weeding in the Cottage Garden, I saw a flash of white in my peripheral vision head off under a nearby plant. My rational mind woke up and thought it must have been a frog or snake that moved so quickly. I searched for several minutes and found no physical evidence of what I had seen. I know now it was my first acknowledged glimpse of a Nature Spirit. So, one of the first steps in connecting to them is to be in the present moment with your surroundings, working with such joy and concentration that you automatically go into a quiet place of intuitive attention.

ACKNOWLEDGING NATURE SPIRITS

Your Nature Spirits love to be acknowledged even if you haven't *physically* connected to them yet. Honoring these Spirits will make their vibration stronger for you and help you to begin tuning into them. I often honor them by using the Native American tradition of a sprinkling of cornmeal over my plants. Maize (corn) is symbolic of the abundance of the earth.

In Bali and Thailand, the people construct beautifully ornate Spirit Houses for the Nature Devas to live in. They believe it is essential to their happiness and longevity to keep the Spirits of the land happy. Before a home construction has even begun, the Nature Spirits are informed of the changes coming. A Buddhist monk comes to the site bearing a tray filled with food and flowers, and while chanting many prayers of gratitude, makes this offering to the Nature Spirits to allow a home to be built on this site. The monk would then move the tray of food very slowly, Nature Spirits following, to an auspicious area in the yard where the Spirit House would then be permanently placed. The Spirit House must never have the shadow of the house fall on it, and it must be more beautiful and ornate than the owner's home. Offerings of flowers and rice or special foods, as well as prayers, are given to the Spirit House daily to ensure happiness and well being for the business or home. They believe a displaced Nature Spirit can cause challenges in your life and your surroundings.

There are many reasons for acknowledging the Nature Spirits through ceremony. Often, it is when we want to take something from Nature; be it land, food, medicine, or even a living tree.

When I first moved to my home, the twelve acres of land had not been honored with any ceremony, but even more so, it had been abused. The only contact with humans in recent years had been men with chainsaws cutting down the trees. Men cut deep into the woods to make the driveway, the first invasion into its protected depths.

Then there was the clearing of the land for the placement of the house. Because we bought this home three years after it was built, we unfortunately had no influence in its construction. I encourage new homebuilders to honor the land throughout the entire building process. Connect with the Nature Spirits of the land from the first time you visit it, and they will reward you with a smooth and uneventful building experience. Don't connect, and you will feel the resistance in subtle and sometimes major ways.

When we first moved to our home, the land edging the driveway felt very hostile. My then 10-year-old son didn't even want to move here. He said the land felt angry. When the driveway had been built, all the trees cut down were placed in a large pile in a field near the road. By the time we purchased the house, tons of construction debris had been piled there, too: plastic, plywood, lumber and the like. It became an eyesore every time we entered the driveway, reminding me of dead bodies that had never been properly buried. I would look at those dead trees and feel a sinking in my Soul.

We knew we had to do something and that we wanted to do it slowly, because after three years several families of rabbits, and who knows what else had made homes in these construction piles. My husband and I decided to get rid of it one log at a time, for however long it took. He would cut each tree into manageable size pieces, and we would place them in the woods, hidden and able to decompose naturally. He began the work with his chainsaw and made slow but steady progress.

One dreary November day I woke with uneasiness in my heart. Although it had been drizzling lightly all day, my husband decided he would go do

A traditional Spirit House
to honor the Nature Spirits
in Chiang Mai, Thailand

some more cutting on the log pile. As he left the house that afternoon, that familiar feeling of dread returned, and I asked him to be extra careful while he worked. Later that day an accident with his chainsaw occurred. While cutting deep into a log that was lying on the top of the pile, the tip of the saw hit the log below it and kicked back like a powerful fist into his face, knocking him flat on his back. Upset with himself, and in shock, he gathered his belongings and headed back to the house, unaware of how injured he really was.

"Honey, I need you" was what I heard in my office, which is on the lower level of our home. It was in that strained voice of controlled panic, and I knew immediately something was desperately wrong. The voice came from our master bathroom, and as I followed it upstairs, I found him leaning over a sink filled crimson red. He had a blood-soaked towel over his entire face, and I was afraid to ask what had happened, though part of me already knew. "I had an accident with the chainsaw," he said. "Can you still see?" was my first question. Yes, he could still see, thank God, but I wondered how long he would stay conscious. After calling a neighbor to care for our children, I drove him to the emergency room in that determined, calm way that takes over in times of crisis. Four hours and over 150 stitches later his face was finally sewn back together. While he was recovering he joked that he wished Halloween had not already passed, because he would not have needed a costume that year!

Every time I tell that story people gasp and put their hands to their faces as if in protection. There is something very vulnerable about injuries to this part of our bodies where so many sensory organs are located. Years later, he barely has a scar and is grateful for the minimum extent of his injury.

I share this experience to explain how the land can get angry with us and tell us it has had enough in all sorts of ways. I believe the Land Deva was giving us a message loud and clear. NO more chainsaws!!

My husband has since sold his chainsaw and is only armed with a single blade handsaw to do light maintenance. It is much safer and can only do minimal damage.

There was much cornmeal and many prayers given to the land after this mishap. After neighbors and friends learned of the accident, they generously offered to help us clean up the log pile once and for all. We decided to do a slow burn on it, giving those trees back to the earth. On an unusually warm 50-degree New Years Day we gathered together in a community of support to honorably give these trees back to the earth. Interestingly, two fires evolved that day; with the women feeding one and the men feeding the other. I called them, most appropriately, the Yin and Yang fires. Yin is traditionally a feminine receding energy, where Yang is an outward, masculine type energy.

My husband even found the log he had been cutting at the time of the accident, and ceremonially offered it to the fire, saying prayers of forgiveness and gratitude for all that we had learned from his accident. In the evening as the embers still glowed, we wrote down on pieces of paper that which we were ready to release and fed them to the fire, too. I kept vigil over the fires that night, and in the morning they were reduced to pure ash.

That spring, my son and I planted a garden where the burned log piles had been, with a mixture of wild and annual flower seeds. Mother Nature had a plan of her own, and filled in the spot with her much hardier seeds of mullein, pokeweed, mustard, and phlox. So there they were, two small hidden circles of garden, about two feet high, of bachelor buttons, sweet william, coreopsis, and marigold surrounded by five-to-six foot tall giants of the natural and hardy field varieties. I laughed to think I could even begin to plan a garden better than her!

To this day that meadow garden is constantly changing and evolving, and we no longer interfere with our store-bought seeds. I go walking through it often, remembering the accident, the healing of scars, and the gifts that occurred there; the gifts of friendship, and gratitude, and releasing that occurred in this sacred space. It now feels like a sacred burial ground for all the beautiful pines that were sacrificed in order for my home to be built. It also feels like a healing space, where the Spirit of the land and myself finally put down our barriers and became deep and cherished friends.

CONNECTING WITH THE DEVAS OF YOUR GARDEN

Look deeply into the lovely forms of the flowers and the trees you care for, and you will see the essence of their spirit dance and play as a rarefied white flame within their bodily form. This is the love and the laughter of the Goddess as she smiles upon the Earth, giving charge to her angels and fairies to vivify and create all Nature anew. To open your heart to the fairies, you must nurture feelings of wonder, reverence and love for every detail of your garden, for the airs which blow about it, the musical rain which falls gently upon it, the high-riding storms which cause its spirit to resonate with the mighty spirits of the elements, the moon and the stars which silently look down on it, the great sun which is the source of its being, and for the clouds and the changing skies which provide it with a canopy. When you can truly feel the sweetness of this magic, you will begin to discover the fairies, for they will make themselves known to you.

SARAH GREAVES

FORBIDDEN AREAS

It is helpful to create an area on your property for the Nature Spirits or Devas that is off-limits to human manipulation and interaction. This area can be roped off or marked with colored flags to remind family and friends it is private ground. This token symbol of respect for the Devas acknowledges your belief in their existence, and provides them with a natural area from which to build their energies. This Forbidden Area, as we call it at our home, is located in a low, wooded valley off of the driveway that has always felt off limits to me. It has a strong vibration of wildness coming from it, and is a place I often leave offerings of cornmeal or flowers from my garden.

My young daughter feels drawn to playing there, and I used to worry that she was trespassing on that special Devic land, and warned her that she should stay off. The Nature Spirits then told me that children are welcome, as long as they are not destructive. I often see Jessie leaving gifts of flowers or stones to trees in this area, and talking to her "friends" as she calls them.

Every garden needs a wild area, even in the city. Once, at a client's home, I asked her if she had a special area set aside for the Devas. She said, "Yes," and proceeded to show me a neglected corner of the yard filled with garden debris, plastic pots and flat containers, bags half-filled with soil, etc., all covered in a tangle of weeds. I told her the weeds were great, but her human garbage had to go if she truly wanted to honor and work with the Nature Spirits of her land.

I speak with my Landscape Deva often, but especially at the start of a new growing season. One February, on a rather blustery day, I heard a small nudging in my head to go outdoors and take a look at the gardens. For over an hour I wandered from one side of the yard to the other, receiving detailed instructions about which plants needed moving, or dividing, and what to plant in specific areas on the land. The Deva and I had long discussions about improving soil and balancing an over-population of destructive insects. There was so much information it filled up four pages in my gardening journal!

STONE PEOPLE

Just as the land and plants have spirits that you can communicate with, so do rocks. The Native Americans call them Stone People, and revere them for their ancient wisdom and centered-ness. I call them the Rock Devas. I know talking to rocks sounds crazy, but it is really more listening that I do. Why do you think so many people have rock collections? How do those stones end up in your pocket, anyway?

Simple stones provide a beautiful, natural, and energetic edging to garden beds

Living in Michigan and having access to the Great Lakes, I grew up learning how to collect rocks. My mother had floor-to-ceiling bookshelves at home not filled with books but with rocks! On vacation, it is the still the best souvenir one could ask for. A hand-gathered stone holds for me the beautiful energy of the place I wish to remember. Just ask my husband how many rocks he has lovingly relocated for me. Even when we moved into our new home, there were several large rocks he willingly hauled onto the moving truck for me that I could not leave behind. Like accessories for my garden, they travel with me wherever I go.

The incredible energy found in rocks also speaks to me when I am working in the garden. I love to border the perennial beds surrounding our log home with beautiful fieldstones. They have an organic feel that compliments the logs and the natural setting of the woodlands. When using hand-gathered stones for a border, I have found the placement of each one is crucial. If I happen to not listen and place them incorrectly, I am hounded until I find its perfect location.

I once intuitively made a border edge for a garden that resembled a snake. I had amassed a large pile of round fieldstone rocks and placed them in my daughter's wagon to begin construction. With a trance-like focus on my task, I went to the wagon and asked in my mind, "Which stone goes next in the border?" Each individual stone would glow, sparkle, or just be the easiest to pick up as I reached for it. When I had completed the entire edge of this garden hugging my backyard, I stood back and realized that the first stone in the line was larger and had an arrowhead like shape and the final stone was ringed and looked like a rattlesnake's tail. For me the snake is a symbol of transformation and with the new subject of feng shui in my life, that is exactly what I was experiencing that summer.

TUNING INTO YOUR LANDSCAPE DEVA

Because he or she acts like the general contractor for the energies in your garden, the Landscape Deva is the first Nature Spirit to begin a conversation with. A simple guided visualization is an easy way to make this connection. You may find it helpful to pre-record the following meditation and play it back to yourself so that you can be fully present with the words you are hearing. It is also really powerful to hear a meditation in your own voice. As you read the words onto your tape, read slowly, leaving some time for visualization between paragraphs and after the questions and experiential statements. Meditation is not to be rushed; it is your personal quiet time. Feel the calm. Also, feel free to adapt the wording so that you are comfortable with the meditation. Make this journey yours, and enjoy.

To begin, find a quiet, comfortable place in your home or outside in your garden, where you know you will not be disturbed for about 20 minutes. It is also helpful to have a notebook and pen handy for taking notes immediately following the meditation, while the information and experience is still fresh in your mind.

LANDSCAPE DEVA MEDITATION

Begin to slowly relax by breathing in deeply through your nose, holding this breath for a count of five, and then exhaling through your mouth. Do this several times until you begin to feel an exhalation, a letting go inside yourself. Sink heavily into what you are sitting on, and have a warm, totally relaxed, clear focus on the present moment. Now in your mind's eye begin to see, sense, or feel the energy of your garden.

Take yourself to a favorite spot, or remember a favorite plant, and begin to sense what its energy feels like. Totally concentrate on just being there. Pay close attention to what is happening around you. Is the sun shining on your skin? Is there a breeze in the air? What does it smell like? What do you hear? Are there birds singing, crickets chirping, frogs croaking? Is water moving somewhere? What do you see? What colors are there? What shapes and textures? Spend some time tuning in to the energy of this place.

As you are present there, a mist begins to roll in at your feet, a beautiful rainbow-colored mist that energizes your entire body. It now covers you from head to toe. Feel the warm pulsing of the colors of this safe, secure blanket of amazing light. Let go and fall into its warm, healing vibration knowing all is well and you are safe in its presence. Now this mist slowly begins to rise and dissipate, and you see or sense your Landscape Deva, standing in front of you smiling, waiting. It may be distinctly a male or female energy, or a blend of both. It could also just be a color or a feeling, but know, in whatever form you sense it, how pleased it is that you want to communicate with it. Co-creating with and teaching humans to remember their connection with Nature, is a joy for them. It is how life used to be in the beginning, when you worked and played so intimately together. Feel this lost piece of you, this old friend, coming forward to be with you again. Take time to acknowledge one another. This is a time of remembering and reconnecting to that ancient relationship.

Now ask this Deva anything you would like to know about your garden. It may be helpful at this time to rise above your home to get a bird's eye view. With your Deva, begin to access your garden from this high vantage point. Feel what areas you are drawn to and begin there. Are there any places that have been neglected? Are there problem areas you would like to focus on? Ask specific questions at this time. Walk around, in your mind's eye, from garden to garden and have conversations with your Deva.

When you have finished, and with gratitude in your heart, say farewell to your Garden Deva. Know that at anytime it is there for you, willing to help you in any garden decisions. It is a part of the land and a part of you, always.

Now begin to focus on your breathing once again, inhaling and exhaling at a rate that feels good to you. Slowly move your fingers and toes, stretch your arms over your head and yawn, bringing yourself back into the present moment, fully alert, feeling energized and ready to go about your day.

Take some time now to write down what information you have received during this meditation.

DUAL COMMUNICATION

Communicating with Garden Devas simultaneously can be a challenging task. Between the Landscape Devas and the Plant Devas, there is a constant dialogue that occurs. Usually I am being told where to place the plant, how deep to plant it, and what prayers to say for its healthy growth. My intuition is open wide to receive these messages, and all of this listening puts me in a deep meditative state concentrating only on the task at hand. It is as if time becomes non-existent. I feel free, relaxed, focused and energized by this experience.

Just ask my family how long I can be in the garden. Often it is ten o'clock and getting very dark outside, and I am still communing with the plants. A good friend of mine just lights some beautiful outdoor candles and keeps on gardening!

When we moved to our present log home, it was from a location less than a mile away. With permission from the buyers, I relocated over 100 perennials from the garden I was sadly leaving behind. The three days it took to "pack" the garden were long and laborious. Speaking with each individual Plant Deva, I asked it if it wanted to be moved, divided, or to stay where it was. There was much dialogue, and I was surprised that only one hundred plants eventually made the trip. These one hundred were all placed in pots and stayed at a neighbor's garden for over a week. To ease their stress and transition, they were watered with a weak solution of the Bach flower essence, Rescue Remedy. Only three plants were lost during this move, while all of the others adapted well to their new surroundings, filling in new gardens that were dug even before inside boxes were unpacked.

CONNECTING WITH THE EARTH AGAIN

A garden planted with intention is more than just digging holes, planting, watering and weeding. It is about creating in yourself the ability to use your human body as a precious link between heaven and the earth. There is a communication, a dialogue that takes place in Nature with our Souls if we but stop to take the time to listen. I believe it is this connection that will not only heal us, but make us wise as well. There is a circle to life, and right now, at this time on earth, we have become the missing piece. In order to take back our rightful and necessary place in the circle, we need to kick off our shoes and feel the *souls* of our feet on the earth again. As kids we loved to get dirty, to roll downhill on the grass, run through the mud puddles, and play in the sand. We grew up and what happened? Appearances became more important than having fun. Clothes took a priority over spontaneity. How did we get so serious? I say it's time to get dirty, have fun again, create new experiences and forget about what the neighbors might say. Here are some earth-connecting ideas to get you started.

- ✥ Choose to walk on the grass rather than on the sidewalk. Revel in the uneven surface and soft textures beneath your feet.
- ✥ Take your shoes and socks off and walk on grass, bare ground, sand, gravel driveways, dry leaves, or moss. Experience the energy that radiates from the earth's surface. Pull it into your physical body through your legs.
- ✥ Pick a wild plant that you know is edible and eat it right from Nature's table. Violet leaves, dandelion greens, and chickweed (pesticide free please) are great plants to start with.
- ✥ Really look at a leaf or a flower for at least one minute straight. Nature does detail like no one else. Sketch it if you want to learn it intimately.
- ✥ Take a walk, not a run, in the rain – without an umbrella or raincoat. Let your face, hair, and clothes get completely drenched. Feel the nourishment of water on your skin.
- ✥ Lay face down in the grass, breathe deeply, then turn over and look up through the treetops to the sky and the clouds. (You did this all the time as a child . . . remember?)
- ✥ Garden without gloves on. Sift the soil back and forth through your hands; let your fingernails get really dirty!
- ✥ Take a fist full of earth and breathe in the ancient aroma. Think about the decaying cycle of all organic matter. This soil was once the living trees, plants, and animals you see around you.

CHAPTER 2

SEASONAL CYCLES
OF A GARDEN

Living in Michigan there is always a distinct cycle to life seen clearly in the growing of a garden. In spring, we wake up the soil from its long slumber, working our energy into the earth and planting the seed. In summer, we lovingly tend and water these young ones, encouraging them, admiring their tremendous growth as the proud parents of our creation. In fall, we begin the process of letting go, putting the garden back to bed, caring for and covering it up with warm blankets of leaves and mulch for the colder days ahead. In winter, we watch as the garden sleeps, knowing there is much still happening beneath the soil. The roots, which are so full of energy, feign hibernation until those first warm days of spring wake them up again.

Swallowtail butterfly on a lilac blossom, the perfect symbol for cycles of transformation

FIRST DAY OF SPRING

The Sun wakes me up,

shining into eyes that wish to stay asleep.

That foggy 'tween place of dreams versus reality.

Why do my dreams always try to lure me back?

Then I hear them. . . .

The dawn chorus of chirping and delight.

Birds, and frogs, and the buzzing of unnamed insects

calling in their own secret language.

One my heart hears clearly,

yet my mind rushes to understand.

"It is Spring – Get out here.

You are missing it!"

MINNIE KANSMAN, APRIL 2000

SPRING

When spring comes to the garden, the gardener is usually more than ready. Like a horse waiting at the starting gate, we burst forth on that first warm day, ready to bring our dreams from the winter into fruition. Just like the plants, we are filled with so much energy and in our urgency to create, also a feeling of there never being enough time to complete it all.

Daylily leaves bursting forth on the first warm days of spring

Spring is the season to take advantage of the cooler weather to labor in, before the dog days of summer come, and all you feel like doing is just admiring your garden from the lounge chair. Remember to pace yourself, to enjoy what you are doing, and savor this time of re-acquaintance and rediscovery for you and your garden. These are often the days I work my back and myself too hard, and my legs complain loudly about my relentless desire to get a head start on the season.

Having grown older, and hopefully wiser, I have learned it is helpful to vary garden chores. For instance weed and deadhead for fifteen minutes, then stand up; walk that refuse to the compost pile. While you are up, treat your spine to a back bend or two to even the score from always bending over forward. Mix some soil and fertilizer in the wheelbarrow, or do some other standing chore, and then go back down to weeding or planting for a while.

While working, I often take a ten-minute sit-down break in one of the many benches or chairs placed strategically around the gardens. This gives me a chance to contemplate and visualize the work I have just completed or the vision I am creating. Stepping back for a moment, seeing the whole picture gives me a different perspective of the project. It also gives me a chance to ask for and listen to the guidance from my Landscape Deva.

Only when I am completely exhausted from my delirium do I grab an iced tea and head for the hammock. Kicking off my shoes, I rock quietly below a canopy of green leaves and relax into the efforts of the day. There is a satisfaction that comes with this kind of physical exhaustion, the kind that only fresh air, dirty hands, clothes, and feet can attest to. It is the feeling of a hard job well done. It is on these nights that I sleep best.

SPRING WARNINGS AND WOODLAND GARDENS

When I was a child, my mother would often take me for woodland walks behind our home. In the early days of spring, we would look for "spring warnings," signals to confirm; that "Yes, the gray days of winter were receding, and the abundance of a new season was upon us."

Often the first shiny green leaves to show in Michigan are from the box elder bushes. Sometimes I pick a bouquet of these twigs to bring home for the table. Emerging leaves; a simple yet perfect sign of what is to come. Other finds could be fresh mushrooms peaking out from under the dry, crackling leaves. The forest in spring is also filled with the sounds of the spring peepers; their percolating songs are music to my ears. How can a creature so small create such a big noise?

True signs of the season are the woodland wildflowers. Spring beauty, trillium, and hepatica are my all time favorites, each possessing such delicate faces opening up to the warmth of the sun. They seem so sweet and fragile looking, yet so brave to be the first on the scene. The wildflower bloodroot fascinates me. An endangered flower now, they grew in abundance near my childhood home. I remember picking them to see the deep red sap drip; imagining it was really blood. Emerging May apples are also a sign in Michigan that cold weather is behind us. With their large, palmate leaves, they make perfect umbrellas during a warm spring rain. I know, because as children, my best friend Kim and I did just that.

I have a shady woodland garden at my home filled with these heralders of spring. Assorted ferns and hosta, bleeding heart, and pulmonaria accompany them. This garden is the easiest one to care for, and the most content. I believe it is because the twelve acres we live on are located deep in the forest. These are native plants that know how to grow best in this specialized environment. Because of this arrangement, Nature literally takes care of this garden for me.

SUMMER

Summer is the active, Yang time of year in the garden. Just keeping every plant fed, watered, and weeded is a full time job. What I relish most about summer though is actually spending time enjoying the garden. To ensure that I do this, a good friend and I have become garden buddies. Once or twice a month we take turns working in each other's garden together. This idea started when my friend Mimi moved into her first home, inherited an already established garden, and had no idea what to do with it. Realizing that I would know, she offered to help work in mine in exchange for teaching and guiding her. We soon discovered how much two pairs of hands could do side by side and how much fun it can be, too.

We often start the day by taking a garden tour, discussing what we would like to accomplish. This helps to keep us on track and focused to the tasks at hand. Then we break for lunch, which has become an important part of the ritual. The food is always healthy, colorful and alive with energy. We attempt to incorporate something grown in the garden with each meal, be it dried herbal tea in the winter or red ripe tomatoes and peppers in the summer. We also always try to eat outside in the garden, weather permitting.

Minnie sharing a garden salad outdoors at the home of her "garden buddy"

Having someone that knows your garden almost as intimately as you is helpful as you make decisions about changes or expansions. They are great springboards to fly ideas off of. What fun you can have shopping together at the greenhouse for plants! They know exactly the spot you are wishing to fill with the plant you are purchasing. In the five years we have been doing this; Mimi has become an amazing gardener. An artist by trade, she brings a special eye to the garden, and I have found that I have learned so much from her. She has taught me a lot about color and form. It is a special friendship, connected through our gardens, and our love for them and each other.

VACATIONS AWAY FROM THE GARDEN

Whenever I am absent from the garden for more than a day, I begin to miss it like an old friend. I wonder what is happening while I'm gone, what burst of growth will I not witness. One practice I have started that helps is to take a little of the garden with me when I go. I pick myself a large bouquet of flowers, grasses and herbs. My favorites are oriental lilies, whose buds are just about to open and I'm certain I will miss their blooming while I am gone. They fill the car with delightful fragrance and often cause a lot of conversation when seen on the picnic table at the campground, or carried through a hotel lobby.

I learned this lesson from a David Austin rose I once had, which would always bloom over the same two-week period in July when we always go camping in Rocky Mountain National Park in Colorado. I would leave at the time it was just starting to show tiny pink buds, and come home to a scattering of soft pink petals on the ground around the base of the plant. It was heart wrenching; I had never seen it in full bloom!

Now I take what I can with me, it has become a habit and tradition. Even for a day trip I may pick a sprig of lavender or mint to place on the front dashboard of the car. As it dries, the aroma fills the air. Coreopsis makes a nice bookmark, as does my favorite, a single sage leaf.

I also have this habit of being a self-appointed, substitute gardener wherever I find myself. Like a duck out of water, I have to find other places to play. Much to my family's dismay, I have been caught picking spent daylily flowers from rest area parking lots, cleaning up the geraniums outside restaurants and gas stations, and watering green plants in hotel lobbies. Like I said before, they call out to me and I cannot ignore their pleas!

One summer we rented a newly built cottage on Lake Michigan for a week. Fresh soil with just a handful of grass seedlings surrounded this beautiful log

Have flowers,
will travel

home. During our peaceful time there, I planned and planted in my mind all the perennial beds I would have placed there, and even what I would put in the non-existent window boxes! I become restless without my hose and pruning shears. Tending garden is such a relaxing part of a summer's day for me. It is why we have warm weather, to grow things!!

AUTUMN

Fall is a glorious time in Michigan. The color show is spectacular, and when the sun is shining it is as if God's own light is illuminating His masterful creations. Sometimes I take it for granted, thinking that everyone gets to experience brilliant ruby-colored sugar maples and blinding golden sassafras. The most memorable are those amazing trees that will hold the colors of green, yellow, orange, black and red all in a single tapestry.

Fall leaves with an icy frosting on a crisp November day

Fall is also the time to plant spring bulbs, which I do with an optimistic heart. What a study in faith it is to spend money on ugly little bulbs, hoping and praying that they will survive the winter and the chipmunks. Yet procrastination is often the name of the game when it comes to actually planting them. The photos at the garden center are all so captivating. Every year I intricately plan out the timing of my Spring Spectacular show. Early blooming tulips with late blooming daffodils; it sounds good, yet rarely do they arrive on cue. Mother Nature has her own plan, depending on rainfall and spring temperatures, and I can only sit back and say I did my part by finally getting them into the ground before snowfall.

Fall is about slowing down and looking within. Like the element of metal, it is a condensing period. It is the best time to evaluate all that has happened in the previous growing season. Take a walk around the yard with pen and paper. I have a specific gardening journal I use year round for this purpose. Write down what did and didn't work.

↬ What was your most spectacular garden memory from the summer?
↬ What was your biggest challenge?
↬ What plants outdid themselves?

↬ What plants or areas need more attention?

Again, this is a time to connect in meditation, or just verbally, with your Garden Deva. Ask what improvements can be made, where, when, and why. This is often a conversation that takes place as inner dialogue, and is important to write down. You will want to refer to your notes during your winter planning/dreaming sessions. Come spring you will be glad you did.

What is also fun is to look back in your journal to the previous years. Much worry and hard work comes pouring out of the pages, making you appreciate the accomplishments you have made so far.

Autumn also brings with it a shift in temperature; to brisk, cool days that make me relish the warmth of the sun even more and appreciate the wool sweater I tossed on.

As a gardener in Michigan, fall colors and warm sweaters are the only positives memories this season brings for me. After the first hard frost, when impatiens and begonias turn into oozing black piles of mush, I go into gardener's withdrawals. Seeing my precious "friends" of the summer season succumb to the bitter cold leaves me sad and depressed. Knowing it will be at least six months before another seedling can be coaxed from the ground, I always question each September why I live in such a cold climate. Perhaps a greenhouse would help alleviate these feelings; I'm still trying to convince my husband of this.

Putting the perennials "to bed" with those beautifully colored leaves or pine needles always brings out my motherly instincts. Will they be warm enough this winter? Should I put an extra layer on just to be sure? What about a freezing rainstorm, or worse yet, a mid-winter thaw and freeze? It is best to just turn it over to the land, and know the healthiest will survive. Plants are tenacious and strong-willed, great teachers under adversity.

Every year I surrender again to the fall. I let go of my strong hold on the garden, relinquishing the sustaining energy of the plants as it travels beneath the earth's surface to concentrate in the roots, and on surviving. Our relationship ebbs and flows; it feels almost as if the plants have gone on holiday and I am awaiting their return in the spring.

WINTER

Winter is dreaming time, when all your grand ideas are played out in your mind and on paper in technicolor, the gardens of Monet and glossy catalogues all rolled into one. You plot how this next year it will all be even grander than the year before. And mistakes from last year are under your belt, not to be repeated. The tomatoes will grow so big, the sunflowers so tall and sturdy. There are no pests or disease in this garden dream. It is only filled with awesome flowers that bloom continually and are the envy of all your neighbors; blooming in soil rich with chocolate brown organic matter, a regular playground for the earthworms. All of nature is happily balanced, and this fantastic garden is an outward expression of that.

Winter, a quiet, inward, Yin time, is the most important time for a gardener. This is when the garden of our dreams manifests itself: nothing is impossible, cost is not a factor, neither is our time or labor. It is as if we have in our possession a magic garden wand . . . and poof it all appears!

This creative and open time is the best time to begin drawing pictures of your dream gardens, labeling the plants you have chosen and writing it all down. Come spring you will be in the more active energy of hands-on doing, ready to finally get outside and feel the soil beneath your feet and in your fingernails, and manifest your plans.

I have created many gardens in the winter this way. Friends say I have a knack for visualization. I can see a complete garden in my mind before it is physically there. I don't think this is a talent only for a few. Through dreaming and drawing, anyone can do it. And, your drawings do not have to be landscape architect perfect either. Mine look very much like chicken scratch, the plants represented by simple shapes and lines.

I often draw a ground level planning sketch and an aerial view. This planning sketch lets me see what it will look like from my visual viewpoint and shows height relationships. The aerial sketch is used to label the plants, and decide how many are needed to fill the space.

An electric heater keeps water available for the birds all winter (the fish like it too)

FEBRUARY IN MICHIGAN

So busy in my mind,
Filled with new ideas
Inspiration that comes
in the dark stillness under the winter's cold blanket of snow.
As I sit, warm and toasty inside
looking out from under the afghan,
soft cat body for a heater by my side.

Dreaming of the Sun
and the
Color Green
— so many shades —
all a welcome relief from the white and gray
that is my current palette.

Dreaming, scheming, wishing, hoping
for that first warm day.
That first shovel full of soil
That smells like caves and mysterious wombs deep in the
Earth.
So impatient I can barely stand it. . . .

MINNIE KANSMAN, WINTER 2000

Sample planning sketch of bench & garden

It is all very loose and flexible. I have discovered that placing the hardscape features first, such as benches, large stones, and walkways helps to create a visual starting point. They provide the garden with visual weight, anchoring it to the ground. Likewise, developing a garden around or next to a large tree creates this balance in a similar way.

All of this brings us back to spring again, and the cycle continues. A delightfully warm spring day is more deeply cherished for having lived through the cold gray days of winter. I am forever grateful for the distinct seasons we experience here in Michigan. Each is a celebration of the passing of time, and honored in its own right.

CHAPTER 3

EXPLORING
GARDEN FENG SHUI

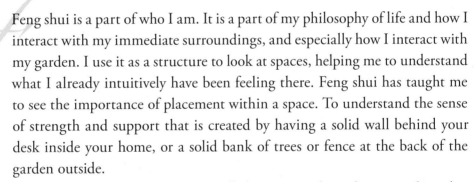

Feng shui is a part of who I am. It is a part of my philosophy of life and how I interact with my immediate surroundings, and especially how I interact with my garden. I use it as a structure to look at spaces, helping me to understand what I already intuitively have been feeling there. Feng shui has taught me to see the importance of placement within a space. To understand the sense of strength and support that is created by having a solid wall behind your desk inside your home, or a solid bank of trees or fence at the back of the garden outside.

Feng shui is about tuning into all that surrounds us, knowing that what we are surrounded by affects us deeply. Our mood, energy level, and even our health are influenced more than we realize by the spaces we occupy. True feng shui is the study of how we, as humans, interact with everything in our environments, and how to optimize those interactions.

A dark and dingy hotel room can leave us feeling sad and lonely. One filled with fresh flowers, blooming plants, and sunshine gives us a feeling of safety and comfort. In the garden, a dark shady corner can feel stagnant and cold. Planting a woodland garden there with delicate green ferns and sweet

Homestead Resort, Virginia
With the correct design we
can direct the path of Chi
in outdoor environments

smelling wildflowers will transform that same area into something beautiful and inviting.

Learning how to make these transformations becomes easy once you understand the basic principles of feng shui. I use feng shui as a fantastic tool to teach others how to increase the beauty and intention of their gardens. And the first step is to get a firm grasp on the concept of energy flow. In feng shui this is called Chi.

CHI FLOW

Chi is the life force that surrounds us all. It is in the atmosphere of our planet, and cycles down to the earth's surface, embracing us with a blanket of energy. This is the Chi force that affects our immediate environments and enters our homes and gardens to breathe life into them. The sacred feeling of being in a pine forest at daybreak, or watching the perfect ease of a sunset as it sinks into the ocean; these are positive ways Chi in which moves in Nature. And when this movement of Chi is unhurried, gentle, and welcoming, our personal Chi – that life force within each one of us – is also nourished.

WIND WATER CHI FLOW

The Chinese translation of feng shui is literally wind and water. If we can imagine Chi as moving like wind or water over the landscape, we can begin to get a sense of what it may also look like. Wind can be felt on the skin, our highly tuned sensory organ that helps us to decipher easily between a gentle breeze and a gale force. Sand or snow carried by the wind gives us a visual aid into imagining what Chi looks like. Chi encircles us like the wind, maneuvering easily around anything in its path. Natural wind blocks, like trees or buildings, help to slow fast moving Chi down to a more healthy and meandering pace. Wind is also a great teacher of where the Chi may be too Yin, or too stuck. A dark, secluded corner may feel like a protected area, yet with nothing growing there it easily becomes neglected, forgotten. It may become a catchall for debris, and usually provides the perfect haven for spiders. In fact, one of my cures for spiders is to hang a Chi generating wind chime nearby. Spiders seem to dislike the constant sound vibration and movement of Chi the wind chime provides.

The flow of water is another visual which can help us "see" Chi. Flooding your garden, in your mind's eye or literally, is a great way to see the Chi present there. The initial flow would come strongest from the main entrance to the yard, usually your driveway. Then it would begin to meander from area to area depending on the grade and slope of the land, and also by what is planted there. A bank of shrubs or large trees would redirect the Chi to other areas in the garden. That steep slope off the back of your yard could have quite an energetic waterfall raging down it. Likewise, a low Yin area of the yard would collect the water and stop its movement. Paths that curve and flow would direct the Chi to curve and slow down, as well. This gentle meandering flow of energy is what you are looking for.

Chi generally moves one of three ways in our garden spaces, meandering, fast, or not at all. This flow can be redirected and manipulated easily by man-made placements. Roads are fantastic examples of how we manipulate Chi. Straight and fast, or curving and slow, our streets set up their own patterns of energy movement. We can do this in the garden with the paths we build, and the garden shapes we design. In the garden, pathways become the roads that move Chi from one area to another. Do you have a dark or gloomy area of your yard where you would like more energy and growth? Create a path of some kind to direct Chi there. You will be surprised at the difference it will make! On the following page are examples of how Chi often flows in our outdoor spaces.

1. Meandering Pattern. Chi moves in a free-flow, meandering pattern, nourishing each and every inch of the garden in a slow, yet energizing, pace. This is the ideal movement you are seeking.

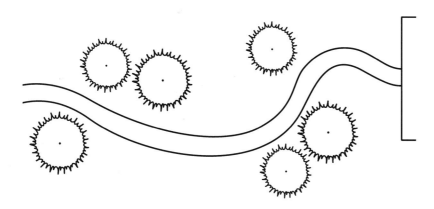

2. Quick Chi. The Chi enters the garden and immediately finds an exit point or drains away down a steep slope. The energy is not around long enough to nourish anything. Humans in this space may feel rushed and anxious, and plants grow poorly and are under stress.

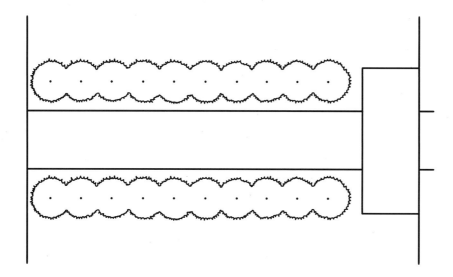

3. Stuck Chi. Chi life force enters a garden space and is immediately absorbed by piles of clutter, junk, or dead and dying plants, or it is blocked in some way. Humans in this type of environment can feel dragged down, tired, and depressed. Plants lack vitality and are susceptible to insect and disease infestation.

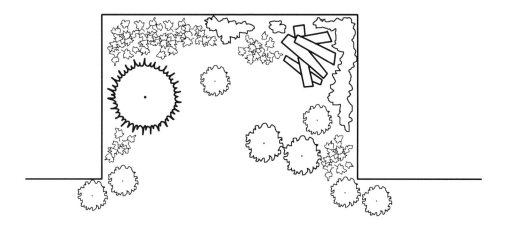

Your driveway in feng shui is known as the Mouth of Chi for your property and the main artery from which this life force enters your land. Let's evaluate how your driveway – its shape, length, and width – affect the movement of Chi to your property. Is the driveway long and straight, heading directly into your garage? Or, does it curve easily and have some hills to move the Chi up and down? The second will have a more relaxing effect on your personal Chi as you wind yourself home from a busy day in the world. It will also bring a softer quality of Chi to your home and gardens. If it is short and straight, there are some adjustments you might consider to slow the Chi down, and make your arrival more enjoyable. For example, adding a lamppost near the road will attract attention there, slow down the flow, and also give support for a climbing plant to grow on. Likewise a small entrance garden anchored with an ornamental tree or large boulder could have the same effect.

The key to evaluating Chi is first understanding it, and then learning how to get it to flow the way you wish. Garden structures, furniture, walkways, and where they are placed, all affect this unseen energy on your property.

Let's look at an example of Chi flow from my own property. The Wealth corner of my present home (you will learn about where your Wealth area is in the next chapter), is on a steep hill that slopes quickly away from the house. In order to "catch" this life force energy and send it back toward the house I intentionally placed an abundance garden there. It is a kidney shape that hugs the house like an open purse, retaining all the money Chi that had previously been flowing down the hill. Finances have been steadily improving since this placement.

YIN AND YANG

In the United States, Yin and Yang are words that have become popular; yet it is a concept that western minds sometimes have difficulty understanding. We often think so linear, everything is either black or it is white. When I first asked my own daughter her definition for Yin and Yang she said, "Mom, it's easy. One side is good and the other side is evil. It's the dark against the light." Praising her for having such a clear opinion, I also let her know there was a more complex layer to this concept of balance.

Yin, like the night, is forever changing with the arrival of the dawn. Yang, the bright expanse of daylight, is always steadily moving towards the dusk. Days are constantly becoming longer or shorter. The seasons cycle around us, as we on planet Earth cycle through the universe. There is a harmonious dance taking place every day in everything surrounding us. It is the Yin Yang dance of life – and it truly is what makes our world beautiful and ever changing.

This flow can be appreciated through exploring more deeply the concepts of Yin and Yang and how they are woven together in this soundless music. Studies have shown evidence that we as human beings desire to be in environments that consist of both Yin and Yang. In fact, these are the places in which we thrive best. For example, building a home in the Yang environment of a hot desert or the Yin of a dark wetland is not as ideal as a home in a sunny location with large shade trees and a source of water nearby. In the desert we crave shade and water. In the wetland we desire the stability of solid ground and the sun.

Feng Shui Master Professor Thomas Lin Yun describes an ideal building location, one where humans would thrive, with the use of this Chinese couplet.

Warm Sun

Gentle Breeze

Lush Trees

Cool Water

Having a balance of both sun and shade, dry and wet appeals most to our sense of well being. Creating a balance of Yin and Yang in the garden makes for smooth Chi flow, good feng shui, and places where we want to spend time.

YIN

Yin is that calm centered feeling of sitting in quiet meditation. It is the opalescent smooth light from a full moon in winter. It is the cool shade under pines on a summer's day. These examples are all holding the energy of Yin: slow, peaceful, night, inward reflection, and quiet shelter. A time to retreat, to assess and sleep, to gather and rebuild, to feel power in the dark thoughts of contemplation and wonder. Yin is soothing and essential, a time for regeneration and rebirth. Without the process of Yin, we would feel hurried and scattered, and eventually burn ourselves out.

Yin energy is inward, quiet, and contemplative like this Buddha wrapped in a snow blanket

YANG

Yang is the active energy of our passions. It is what propels us to move forward in life. It is the hot sun shining down on a blinding white sandy beach. It is large and solid surfaces, like skyscrapers or immense rocks. Yang is also present in vibrant hues that attract our attention, like the glowing oranges, and bright yellows of tuberous begonias, or the upward thrusting sheaths of exotic red cannas. Anything full of energy and quick moving, even animals and people are all Yang elements. Without Yang life would come to a standstill and nothing would ever be motivated to move forward.

Colorful hanging fuchsia brings bright fiery Yang energy to the garden

In the garden, Yin and Yang energy are manifested in these components:

YIN	YANG
Moon	*Sun*
Earth	*Sky*
Winter	*Summer*
Cold/Cool	*Hot/Warm*
Wet	*Dry*
Small	*Large*
Ornate	*Plain*
Horizontal	*Vertical*
Plantings	*Statuary*
Perennials	*Annuals*
Shady areas	*Sunny Areas*
Pastel, receding colors	*Bright, vibrant colors*

As I said before, humans thrive in an environment that consists of a balance between these two opposing forces. We enjoy being on a sunny patio that still offers areas of respite under a cool umbrella. We love spending a cold winter's night curled up by the warm glow of a fireplace. We want and need them both. The extreme of either independently causes discomfort, which in turn creates less desirable feng shui.

This desire for balance is so profound that most elements, especially those found in Nature, are comprised of a mixture of Yin and Yang. Take, for example, a Queen Elizabeth rose. It is predominately Yin energy, because it is a green plant with pastel pink blossoms that are very frilly and ornate. However, the fiery sharp thorns and vertical shape of this rose also give it a strong Yang element.

Take an overall assessment of your garden and see whether it is predominately Yin, Yang, or a nice balance of the two. Do you love the intense shades of orange and red? A garden filled with only these colors, in a hot sunny location, can begin to feel dry and unwelcoming. Add a water feature, like a birdbath or a shady gazebo, and the area becomes instantly more inviting.

Do you have a dark and shady corner under the eves of your home that is constantly wet? Add a statuary piece, like a Buddha or angel, some ferns and white flowers, and feel it transform into a shrine.

Professor Thomas Lin Yun says, "Where a green plant thrives, so does a human." Making garden spaces that fill this need for Yin and Yang create beautiful and comfortable environments for Souls.

APPLYING FENG SHUI TO YOUR GARDEN

When I began studying feng shui the first question I asked my teachers was, "How do I apply this to my garden?" I instinctively knew that the energies that surrounded a house were just as, if not more, important to pay attention to as those inside. This is, after all, where true feng shui began; as a method of calculating the most favorable positions to site homes and graves. What you first see as you walk toward your home or building will have a great influence on your experience inside.

Applying feng shui principles to your landscape is very easy. First, decide how the Chi, or life force energy, is entering your property. Then determine the exact footprint or shape of your property. Next, you are gong to overlay the bagua map onto this footprint. With this information, you can easily determine if you have any missing area of the bagua, enhancements, or places that need the Chi flow adjusted.

Chi flow usually enters your property from your driveway or main entrance to your plot of land. The exception will be if you live on a lake, as a huge amount of energy will be coming from this natural source. One of the most intriguing Japanese gardening stories I have heard is about a gentleman gardener whose home faced the ocean. He created a beautiful garden in his backyard and had a 10-foot fence constructed to enclose it and to block the ocean view. In the middle of this fence a large round moon gate opening was placed. This way the Chi came slowly and deliberately into his garden. The view of the ocean was a complete and wonderfully unexpected surprise to his guests, and his gardens were fully appreciated.

To be able to lay the bagua map out over your property, an accurate copy or drawing of the shape of your lot is necessary. A copy of your property survey can often be found in your home mortgage papers. Once you have this important diagram, the fun begins!

The Basic Bagua

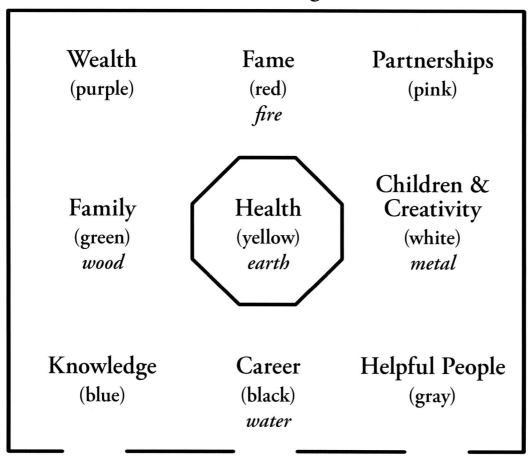

Wealth
(purple)

Fame
(red)
fire

Partnerships
(pink)

Family
(green)
wood

Health
(yellow)
earth

**Children &
Creativity**
(white)
metal

Knowledge
(blue)

Career
(black)
water

Helpful People
(gray)

Mouth of Chi

APPLYING THE BAGUA MAP

Ba means eight and *gua* means sides in Chinese, and the original bagua is an eight-sided figure, with the center of this octagon being the ninth area. I work with a bagua map that is square in shape, the corners of the original octagon have been pulled out to create a square, which is much easier to lay over site plans.

The bagua is an ancient feng shui tool that utilizes the placement of what are called the nine life conditions. These are the areas of our life where we expend our time and energy. They are also often referred to as guas. When used in feng shui, the bagua grid is laid out over your landscape plan to determine the placements of these nine life conditions. Divide your property up into nine equal pieces, and lay the bagua map over the diagram. When looking at your overall yard or landscape, aligning the front edge of the bagua with the driveway entrance will always put the front edge of your lot in the Knowledge, Career, or Helpful People gua.

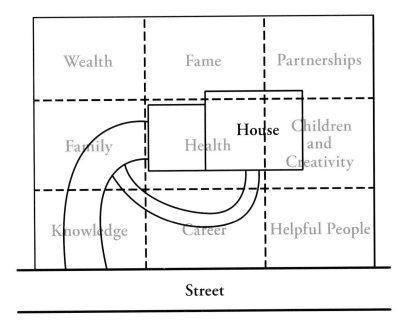

Bagua Overlay on Property

You may also choose to look at the bagua placement over an individual garden, or the gardens surrounding your home. I call the bagua the *ever-shrinking, ever-changing bagua* as it shrinks and grows according to the individual area to which you apply it. In the landscape it can be applied over your site plan, the immediate garden space around your home, just your front yard or just your back yard, and even separate freestanding gardens, like a vegetable patch. Here are some examples:

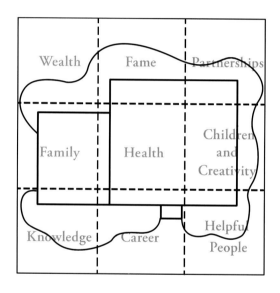

Overlay on Gardens

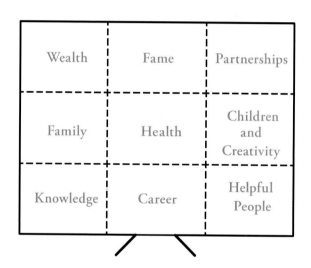

Overlay on Specific Garden

MOUTH OF CHI

To decide where to place the outer edge of the bagua on these free standing spaces, it is important to determine what is called the *Mouth of Chi*. The Mouth of Chi in your garden is the entrance you use most often to access it. It is called the mouth because this is the place where the largest amount of Chi, or life force energy, flows into it that space. Think of it as the main doorway to your garden, which is like a living breathing creature that is fed from the vitality of Chi that immediately surrounds it.

FINDING THE MOUTH OF CHI

Where does the major influx of energy flow into your space? If you are studying the overall property of your lot, the Mouth of Chi is your driveway entrance. If you wish to concentrate on your front yard only, it is usually the beginning of the sidewalk leading to the front door. In the backyard, the entrance is determined by how you gain access most often to this area. It is usually from a back door, back porch deck, or sliding doors from the house. If there is no back door, only side doors from the house, or the garden is free standing, then use the route you walk most often to enter this garden.

OVERVIEW OF GARDEN BAGUA LAYOUT

- Find the Mouth of Chi entrance to the garden area you are working with.
- Overlay the bagua on your garden with the Knowledge, Career, and Helpful People areas always situated along the front edge at this Mouth of Chi.
- Divide the garden into nine equal areas.
- These nine areas become the nine life conditions.

THE NINE LIFE AREAS OF THE BAGUA

After figuring out the placement of the bagua over your chosen garden, you can easily see where the nine life areas or guas are located. These areas have certain attributes that help to define the energies of each space.

Family represents your immediate family, and also any human support system you may have such as a spiritual study group, sports team, or even beloved ancestors that have passed on. The color green, spring, and new beginnings symbolize this area. It is the active element of rising wood, strong and stable, a pioneer energy. The shape here is columnar, like a tree. It provides the ability to move forward with strength from the past, yet also knows how to bend in the wind, instead of being brittle and breaking.

Wealth represents material and spiritual wealth, a peaceful sense of well being. It is a feeling of being blessed with more than enough, that life is full to the brim and overflowing. This gua is energized by the elegant color of purple. The wood element also stimulates this gua.

Fame describes how you are seen by others and also by yourself, your reputation in life or life resume. It is illumination: how brightly do you shine? The element that activates this area is fire and the color red. Strong bold lines and triangular shapes are associated with fame. The season is summer with all of its passion.

Partnership speaks about learning to live in a close, intimate relationship with yourself and one other person. Mother and child, husband and wife; all are mirrors to help us see who we are more clearly. All shades of pink, peach and beige are used here. Earth is the element used to ground this energy.

Children and Creativity represents anything you would like to nourish and grow, such as future plans, projects, and/or kids. It is about completing those projects with joy in our hearts, and also influencing others with our ideas and creativity. The colors used here are white and pastels. The element is metal; the season is autumn; a time of harvest, feeling full, complete, refined, and clear. Round and oval shapes and arches are used here.

Helpful People is associated with heaven and all otherworldly assistance. Angels, guides, guardians, and totem animals are all helpful beings in your life. So are the plumber, your best friend, your feng shui consultant, and anyone who comes to your aid in times of crisis. The colors associated with this area are gray and silver. The metal element enhances this gua.

Career represents your life's path or journey. What did you come on this earth to accomplish? The elemental energy of water is held here, especially deep, moving water, which is our social connection to the world. The color black here symbolizes that deep pool of reflecting water that helps us contemplate our purpose. Free form, undulating shapes best symbolize this water area.

Knowledge represents the ideas of true wisdom, life experience, and inner knowing. It is the ability to use our spiritual insights and intuition to help us understand life, to find our own answers within. The element of earth helps to keep one centered during this process. The colors used here are shades of blue and blue-green.

Health energy is held in the center of the space, it truly represents a balance of Yin and Yang. Health is physical, emotional, mental, and spiritual well being. Perfect health is achieved when the Chi flow of all the eight surrounding guas are balanced. Its colors are the earth tones of gold, orange and bright yellows.

ENHANCEMENTS AND MISSING AREAS

Most of us do not live with perfectly square or rectangular houses, lots, or even gardens. When you lay the bagua map over these spaces, sometimes there are areas that protrude from the main layout. These protrusions are called enhancements. Enhancements are great, and offer additional energy to the section of the bagua they support.

Conversely, if you lay the bagua map over your home or property, and it appears to have holes or open areas, these are called missing pieces. Here is a general rule to follow: if what is protruding out from the bagua overlay is less than half of the total length of that side of the area, it is an enhancement. If what is protruding out is more than half of the total side of that area, it creates a missing piece.

In feng shui we are most concerned with correcting these missing areas. Having a missing area on the bagua is akin to having a treasure chest filled with abundance, and no room to store it in. Below is a diagram of a missing area in wealth for a home and for its property.

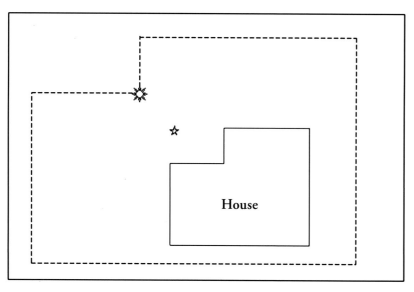

Sketch of Missing Areas in Wealth

Key

✹ Transcendental cure placement: wind chime, crystal

✩ Mundane and/or Transcendental cure placement: tree, statue, rock, birdbath, garden

There are several practical ways to adjust these missing areas. In feng shui these are called mundane cures, which are the simple adjustments that one might first think of, such as filling in a missing area with a garden or deck. Anchors, which physically hold or weigh down an area, are also used to complete a missing space. An excellent example of a visual anchor is a flowering tree that blooms in the corresponding color of that missing area of the bagua. The tree is planted at the spot where, if the space had been whole, the edges would have aligned. (See small star on diagram.) Anything heavy and permanent like a large rock or piece of statuary also works well here.

A common feng shui adjustment is to bury symbolic stones to anchor these missing areas. Because of their corresponding color to the gua areas, amethyst works well for Wealth, rose quartz for Partnership, sodalite for Knowledge, and clear quartz can be programmed for any area. When people balk at burying such a beautiful stone, I remind them they are returning it back to the earth from where it originally came. When they ask how large a stone to bury, such as an amethyst, I reply, "How much wealth do you want?" My usual recommendation is at least a fist size piece.

There is an important lesson in learning this give away back to the land, and also a magical element in knowing you have "buried treasure" in your back yard. When making a hidden adjustment, such as burying a stone, I also recommend an aboveground placement such as planting a tree or placing a statue. This overlapping of adjustments makes them even more powerful.

If you have a missing piece of the bagua on your lot, and the area needing to be filled in is not on your property, transcendental cures are needed. (See large star on diagram.) A transcendental cure is one that uses symbolism and an active visualization from you to hold its energy in place. For example, my property has a large missing piece in wealth. When we first moved here, expenses to just operate the house seemed astronomical and it felt like there was no room to hold our treasure in; it was flowing out the door too quickly! After a year, much to my pleasure, I recognized this gaping hole in wealth on my lot survey. I had been too busy with the feng shui of the house's interior to see it before. So that winter, in over 4 feet of snow, I sat on my husband's shoulders and tied a 40 mm clear round quartz crystal in a tree at the lot line's corner. (See diagram.) This round cut crystal shines its light evenly out in all directions. And, with my visualization, it shines out to energetically claim this portion of my neighbor's land, which happens to fill out my missing Wealth area, even as the land is still physically his.

Every time I walk by this crystal hanging in the woods, I visualize the expansion of my Wealth area taking place here. Sure enough, the utility bills became more reasonable, and the money started flowing in to keep up with our expenses. We were even able to begin saving more! A wind chime could also be substituted for this adjustment, visualizing the sound traveling out to fill in the missing area.

CHAPTER 4

FENG SHUI ADJUSTMENTS
FOR THE GARDEN

ॐ

There are many ways to apply the rules of interior feng shui to the outdoors. Without any feng shui garden books available when I began to study these principles, my first exterior placements were based on pure experimentation. An avid gardener at the time, I took what I had learned from interior adjustments and began applying them to 'outdoor rooms.' Feng Shui placements create physical results because that they are reminders of our intentions. As my teacher Denise Linn always says, "Where attention goes, energy flows!" The basic tools of feng shui, which help to move and direct the energy of Chi flow, are as follows.

LIGHT REFRACTING OBJECTS

A gazing ball placed in the wealth corner of a lot becomes the focal point of an abundance garden

This category includes outdoor lighting, mirrors, and crystals. These man-made items have the ability to attract Chi, to redirect it, and/or to keep it flowing in a specific direction.

LIGHTING

Adequate lighting is essential to attract the positive flow of Chi to your home, and most importantly to the walkway and front entrance. *Miss Chi* likes to be able to find your house just as easily in the dark as during the day. Make sure all entry lights are functioning properly with no bulbs burned out. When a bulb does burn out, replace it as quickly as possible. At our home we live by the 48-hour-rule. All burned out bulbs must be replaced within 48 hours from the time they were first noticed. This helps to keep a positive energy pattern flowing with no disruptions.

Because lighting sends Chi out in all directions equally, it is an excellent way to fill in a missing area of the bagua. Installing a lamp post or spot light at the outside corner of an incomplete area fills that space with light, thus symbolically filling it with Chi and creating a balanced building. The lights do not need to be on all the time to do this work. Having an electricity source running to the lamp, and a working switch to activate it are all that matter.

As for garden lighting, my favorite form is natural candlelight. With so many beautiful garden torches and candle stakes available to purchase, this is easy. Because I have a July birthday, we often celebrate it in the garden. One year I gave myself a firefly birthday party. That evening, guests sat at patio tables outside that were covered with small containers of flowers and tea lights. Several hanging candle torches and covered lanterns dispersed throughout the garden illuminated the flowers and the frog-filled pond. Tiny fairy lights on connecting strands encircled the entrance and garden archway. The true magic of the evening began as the fireflies came out to play, and danced with the sparkler-waving guests.

When candlelight is not practical, solar or single-spaced spotlights are my next choice. Lighting dispersed to areas where it is necessary for ease and safety, or to highlight the beauty of a particular garden feature are the best placements. Illuminating a hidden walkway, reflecting a pond or water feature, near a back-door entry, or showcasing a specimen tree are all good uses.

My least favorite types of outdoor lighting are individual low voltage lights that flank either side of the walkway like soldiers. These airplane runways move

Electrical lighting in a Japanese lantern is a fun and easy way to create night magic in the garden

the Chi too quickly, usually slamming it into the front door, without spending time in the garden gathering its benefits. This can create a rushed and unnatural feel to the garden, and to those using this path to enter the home.

MIRRORS

The most effective use of a mirror in a garden that I have experienced was at Denise Linn's home. In the outdoor hot tub area is a beautiful metal sun shaped mirror that reflects the lush California wine country behind it. As I used this mirror one morning to brush my hair, I saw the uplifting reflection of my face surrounded by the amazing green colors of the hillside and majestic oak trees. There was my face surrounded by all that beauty. It truly lifted my Chi for the entire day!

Mirrors can also be used to move Chi into a dark corner or otherwise void wall of an out building or fence. It can become a focal point for this space, with plantings or vines added to compliment it. Pay special attention to what is reflected in the mirror. Views of water, such as a lake or ocean, are particularly auspicious. Doubling a view of the garbage cans is not.

There is a traditional feng shui mirror adjustment to implement if you have a large tree planted directly in front of the front door. A tree in this position is viewed as unlucky, as it is blocking the positive flow of Chi from entering your home. To remedy this situation, place two small round mirrors on either side of the tree's trunk at eye level from the front door. This transcendental adjustment creates a porthole for the Chi to now flow easily through the tree and into your home.

CRYSTALS

A tool often used in feng shui is a round faceted cut crystal. Because of their ability to disperse Chi flow in a circular and balanced manner, they can be used to fill out a missing area of the bagua with great results, as previously discussed.

Crystals are also wonderful adjustments for enhancing specific areas of the bagua on your property. If you would like to bring more clarity and understanding to a relationship, hang a round faceted crystal somewhere in the Partnership gua of your garden or land. They look beautiful and catch the light nicely when hanging in a tree. If you would like to connect more intensely with your angels or spirit guides, place one in the Helpful People gua. It is your focused intention when hanging the crystal that programs it, to carry out your desires.

SOUND/WIND CHIMES

Why are wind chimes a highly regarded tool and an adjustment often recommended in feng shui? A metal wind chime sets up a sound vibration that continues to travel forever into the ethers. When you hang a chime for a specific intention, that intention or prayer is sent out into the universe every time the wind blows. By placing a wind chime in a particular location, for example the Career area, you can further enhance this adjustment by setting an intention that this tool will call in a new or better career situation for you. Seeing and hearing the chime ring will help to reinforce this visualization in your own mind of a new and better life path coming forward.

It is best if the chime is made of metal, though I do love the soothing rhythm of a high quality bamboo chime. Bamboo chimes work well in the Family area to call in a peaceful energy for family relationships.

The clapper of a wind chime, the flat piece at the bottom which catches the wind and makes it sound, may also be used to reinforce an adjustment. I often suggest to clients that they write down on a small piece of paper the specifics of what it is they desire, then roll the paper up into a small scroll and attach it with red string just above the clapper. It is then hung in the bagua area of the garden that will lend the most support to their request.

For example, to attract a new relationship you would write down the qualities you are looking for in a partner on a small piece of paper. Make sure you have asked for specifics, such as unmarried, debt free, etc. I have learned from experience that you get what you ask for, or what you forget to ask for!

Roll this list up into a small scroll and tie it above the clapper of a metal

Fountains bring the element of
water and life force into a garden

wind chime with red string. Hang this wind chime in a tree in the Partnership area of your yard. I have had clients use this adjustment with great success. Variations of this idea can be used in the Helpful People gua for hiring new employees, and in the Career gua to facilitate job changes.

WATER GARDENS AND FEATURES

Water is an important element in the garden and an excellent Chi flow generator. It is a pure symbol of life and vitality. Those who have water survive! When placing a water feature in the garden, it is essential that the water remain in motion, otherwise stagnant Chi can develop. The direction of the water flow should always be towards the home, not away from it, unless it is a circular fountain, which generates Chi in all directions. Birdbaths are also the exception, as the birds provide wildlife Chi energy with their bodies and movement.

LIVING OBJECTS

Of course, the plants in your garden are the main living objects that give off life force energy. Birds and animals would also be included in this list. I cannot imagine my garden without the sounds of the birds and the activity they provide. They are especially important in a winter garden to sustain a high level of Chi. Bird feeders, suet cakes, and even an occasional squirrel, all help to feed this energy surrounding your home.

Attracting hummingbirds with a nectar feeder in the summer enables us to experience the magic and joy of these miniature creatures. Butterflies, bees, and the beneficial insects to be discussed later fill a garden with color, movement, and life!

HEAVY OBJECTS

Weighted ornaments such as statuary, fountains, and even natural boulders lend a sense of stability to the bagua area in which they are placed. Because these items are less likely to be moved, they make excellent anchors for missing pieces. Symbolism can be used here as well. For example, I have a Japanese lantern statue that can be lit with a candle thereby anchoring the missing knowledge piece in my garden. Knowledge is about finding the wisdom of your soul, and an image that provides light is perfect for this searching.

Bright colors activate Chi in the garden

COLOR

The use of color in feng shui is a powerful tool, yet some people may become overly focused on it. Using the corresponding color for each gua exclusively in each respective area can create boring and predictable garden spaces. Just as I do not encourage my clients to paint every interior room located in the Wealth gua purple (unless they really love purple and want to), I do not insist they plant only purple-blooming flowers in a Wealth area of their garden. Blossoms in shades of purple, blues, and pinks would be much more interesting. Yet, sometimes an all purple garden *is* just the visual element a client needs to focus intensely on collecting wealth.

Color is one tool of many to be used in feng shui to enhance and activate an area; and activate it will! Color has an immediate effect on our auric field. Those who study color therapy have discovered that the speed of penetration for color is faster than that of sound or movement. Color sends an immediate vibrational message from the object we are looking at through our eyes directly into the brain.

The color red is popular in feng shui because it represents the powerful fire element, and is said to hold the highest vibration for activating that which you are asking for. Like a fire, red brings about transformation quickly. To attract Chi to the front entrance, plant red flowers here or even paint the front door red. If the idea of a red front door is too bright for you, paint it a color that is pleasing to you and enhance the area surrounding it with color; perhaps a

bright doormat that has the red color in it or a colorful wreath you hang on the wall nearby.

OTHERS TO BE DISCOVERED
HANDMADE ITEMS

This is where your personal intention creates the most perfect adjustment for your situation. Tailor-made cures derived from your thoughts and actions are often the most effective ones. For instance, maybe you are a potter and create out of clay your own personal abundance symbol. From the first moment you touched that clay you began to put your positive thoughts and feeling about abundance into this symbol. The creation knew it was to be a symbol for abundance even when it was just a lump of clay because of your initial intentions. What we create with our own two hands is filled with our powerful energy.

USING FLORAL DESIGN PRINCIPLES

In a garden there are many adjustments that come from an understanding of just feeling and knowing what is right for that space. Applying the principles of floral arranging to the much larger outdoor 'container' of a garden, creates the same desired result as a beautiful vase filled with blossoms.

Before I discovered feng shui, I worked professionally for 15 years as a master floral designer. I started studying Botany at Michigan State University, and then quickly became bored with the idea of white lab coats and seed propagation. Sitting in on the wrong class one day, I stayed because the professor was lecturing at length on perennial gardening. Talking to him after class I discovered there was an actual major called Commercial Floriculture, in which I promptly enrolled. How exciting that I could really get a college degree in taking care of and working with flowers!

It was through my floral design studies that I realized planning a garden is like designing a floral arrangement, only on a much grander scale. What is interesting is that the main principles used in floral design apply just as easily to a garden and are as follows: Movement, Balance, Texture, and Focal Point. Paying special attention to these four areas will help you to design an interesting and visually pleasing garden.

MOVEMENT

Color that is spaced throughout your garden helps to create movement there. If you plant only one yellow-blooming flower, it will stand out like a sore thumb. Instead, plant several spaced at intervals, which create a natural visual flow from one area of the garden to another. You can repeat the same plant, or bring in new textures and shades by adding a different, yet similar, yellow bloomer that echoes the original.

For instance, in my Cottage Garden, bright yellow coreopsis bloom at the front edge, while further in the back are lemon yellow lilies that repeat this same vibrant hue, in addition to the shorter yellow golden marigolds dispersed along the walkway. These particular flowers all happen to have the same bloom time, which is important in a perennial garden. Each of these plants has a distinct leaf texture and shape, yet they all have the bright yellow color in common. Dispersing plants like this creates a movement that your eyes follow from one yellow to the next.

Movement is also enhanced by the physical way certain plants move in the wind. The wild grasses have a soft fluid dance, while the bright red crocosmia, with its tall broad leaves, often catches a breeze and vibrates like a drum.

Birds and animals, especially fish and frogs, provide a constantly changing scene in the garden. I love it when I approach the pond on a warm summer day, and almost a dozen frogs jump with a wonderful plip-plop pattern into the water. Then they turn around to stare at me from their new vantage points with questioning eyes about why I disturbed their sunbathing.

BALANCE

Balance can be established in the garden in many ways. One of the easiest is to study the Chinese five-element system, making sure you have all of the elements represented through color, shape, and/or the actual physical element.

Another way to create balance is to compare the amount of hardscape (benches, paths, statuary, fountains, birdhouses, etc.) to softscape (plants, shrubs, trees, grass). Have these items compliment one another rather than overtake each other. Be careful not to go overboard with too much "yard art", such as flags, whirly gigs, and gnome statues. The flowers can get lost in the busyness of all this extra decoration. Likewise, I have also seen a "wild" area of plants suddenly come all together with one perfect statue and a meandering stone path running through it.

Balance can also be established by having several plant heights and shapes in your garden. Low, flat beds of annuals are greatly enhanced by some taller perennials, and perhaps a fence or trellis for vines in the background. Vertical, open-branching trees or shrubs are complimented by mass plantings of creeping groundcovers underneath them. Varying the heights in your garden helps the Chi flow to travel to these levels as well, and makes for a more interesting garden.

TEXTURE

Having a variety of textures in a garden is one of the single most important influences to its success. Variety is the spice of life, and adding variety by leaf and flower shape seasons up a space. Just as it would be boring to have all daisy-shaped flowers planted together, so would a lot of compact round shapes, such as marigolds. Yet, when you plant daisies and marigolds together that is when the space comes alive! I love placing long, slender leaves, like the daylily, next to a soft furry leaf, like lamb's ears. The contrast between the two makes them both stand out. Hosta, with their large, flat, smooth leaves contrast nicely with the refined textures of delicate fern fronds. Roses, with their large open flowers, have always looked great next to the tiny, delicate blooms of baby's breath (*Gypsophila*). Deliberately planting such visually distinct flowers or leaf structures together creates unique and interesting garden designs.

FOCAL POINT

Focal points in the garden are often created by the hardscape already there. In my Cottage Garden the focal is the black, wrought iron archway that is covered with purple clematis and sky blue morning glories. In another area of this same garden, after traveling a winding path, the frog pond becomes a natural stopping point. Birdbaths, fountains, even seating areas are often where our attention travels to first. The flowers become the upholstery, or enhancements, that tie an area together and truly bring it into balance.

Large specimen trees also make a great focal foundation for a garden to rise up from. I spoke earlier about designing a garden around a tree, which serves as its anchor. That is what a focal point is in a garden or in a floral design, the anchor your eye is initially drawn to. Your attention then travels pleasingly around the garden, discovering all its hidden treasures, and then rests peacefully back upon the original focal that caught your eye in the first place.

ADJUSTMENTS FOR SPECIFIC BAGUA AREAS

Each area of the bagua lends itself to individual feng shui adjustments that work well with the energy of that space. Here are several ideas for enhancing each one of these unique areas in the garden.

CHILDREN AND CREATIVITY

This is the area of the garden where you can let your imagination soar! Think like a child again and fill it with your heart's desire. Remember the plants of your youth, the flowers you adored for their intriguing names, like snapdragons, or their heady scents, like lilac or lavender. These are the plants to put in your Children and Creativity garden.

Go wild with color combinations, throwing caution to the wind. My son, at age six, planted the most beautiful shade garden of his own choosing. It had orange and white tuberous begonias, hot pink new guinea impatiens with variegated leaves, and purple blue browalia. It was electric and amazing!

Garden art and sculpture are also fun additions to this creative area. My home has a Fairy Garden in the Children and Creativity area, complete with metal fairy sculptures and hidden beings peaking out from under the hostas. Fairies have deep magical meaning from my childhood and help me to remember and connect back to this elemental world as an adult. Old-fashioned pink foxglove grows here, as well as delicate blue flax, baby's breath, canterbury bells, and lady's mantel. These, to me are "fairy flowers"; magical, sweet, and innocent.

Eastern redbud tree (cercis canadensis) with fairy statue beneath it

PARTNERSHIP

The Partnership area of my garden always seems to need more attention, just like the partnerships in my life. I have a wonderful relationship with my husband. We are both loving and very supportive of each other, yet there is always more work that can be done to make it even better. In my garden in the Partnership gua, there is a slight sloping of the land here, like in the Wealth area, though not as steep. I felt the energy here draining away sometimes, just like it was flowing at times from personal relationships. A tall trellis, placed here for the clematis, did wonders to create a screen to catch this Chi flow, and had an immediate positive effect on my relationships.

There are several pink flowering perennials and shrubs here – phlox, weigelia, wild geranium, and impatiens. Pink tulips and white daffodil bulbs with pink center bloom here in the spring. Do the impatiens symbolize more than I had consciously thought? Did I plant them here to remind me to have more patience in my life with the people that I love?

Recently I acquired an old-fashioned hanging wooden porch swing, perfect for two to sit on. It is hung under the eves of the second-story deck, and provides a wonderful view of this garden, as well as a great place to just sit and talk.

Another hardscape feature deliberately placed here is a hammered metal birdbath, which has perched on its edge two tiny metal birds. Using pairs of

The color pink, and anything in pairs enhances the partnership area

anything, be it figurines, sculptures, or even rocks, helps to feed the partnership energy. This garden is also the home of my "heart rock" collection.

One client I worked with lived in a home where the entire relationship area was missing. Where the Partnership gua of her house should have been was actually outside in a garden area. Interestingly, she had purchased the home for her and her young son shortly after becoming a widow. We are often attracted to spaces that simulate what we are learning at the time. She said her husband's death had left a giant void in her life. Her home, with the missing area in relationship, was mirroring that.

She called me for a feng shui consultation, as she finally felt ready to begin looking for a new relationship. We discussed placing something symbolic in this garden area, and I even suggested naming it the Relationship Garden. Naming inanimate things like homes, cars, and gardens develops an even more intimate connection to them.

My suggested adjustments of a pink climbing clematis or a birdbath to anchor this missing area weren't hitting the mark for her. She then shared she was beginning a sculpture class and asked, "Could I make my own piece of art for this space?" I was thrilled, because I knew this would be the most powerful adjustment of all. As I said earlier, what someone makes with their own hands, while anchoring intentions into it at the time of its creation, always produces amazing results. Shortly after she finished planting her Relationship Garden she began dating again, feeling very comfortable with the process and the ability to move forward in her life.

Another client lived on a lake, and in the Partnership area of her yard she had placed a large bench comfortable enough for two. It had a beautiful garden of light purple coneflowers and pink painted daisies surrounding it. She and her husband often sat there together in the evenings, watching golden sunsets on the water and listening to the purple martins return to the large condo-style birdhouse located nearby on the dock. This bench became an even more sacred space to spend time together after she was diagnosed with cancer. Here they found strength in the beauty of Nature, and in each other, to keep living.

HELPFUL PEOPLE

This area of my home, sandy and barren, was a big missing piece when I first moved in. But often times, the good thing about a missing area in a structure is it creates a natural corner space just waiting to be turned into a garden. That is my favorite cure for any missing area outside: fill it with something green and growing! So I decided to plant my Buddha garden in this space, the focal point of it being a large Buddha statue sitting under a gingko tree. Soft grasses, pastel-blooming flowers, and the herb angelica all add to this helpful people collection. At the exact corner of the missing area, not too far from Buddha, is a round metal sign with the oriental kanji symbol whose translation is "to grow".

While tending this garden I am constantly reminded of the support I receive from all the spiritual benefactors in my life. It also symbolizes for me the role I am actively growing into in becoming a Helpful Person for others in my life. Statues of St. Francis, Mother Mary, or angels are also good placements for this area. A statue gives you the perfect anchor and focal point around which to create a garden.

Because the Helpful People area is always located at the front line of the home on the right-hand side, it may be at your front entry. If not, this area is usually visible from the front entry door and most often the driveway. Seeing your favorite symbol of spirituality and strength upon your first arrival is a wonderful way to be welcomed home.

CAREER

This garden is placed at the center front area of the home and may even be at the entry. This grand exposure gives you the opportunity to tell the world just who you are! Keep this garden area especially well cared for to assist Chi's movement into the house. I find if my business could use a burst of energy, or I have questions about what to do next, I go out and sweep the stone walkway and front porch area that is in the Career gua of my home and garden. While I sweep, I ask for clarity about a Career question or visualize creating an easy path for customers to find me who are in need of

Metal art of the Japanese kanji symbol meaning, "to grow"

my services. Often a client calls as I am returning to the house, or an idea comes easily to me.

If this area is recessed into your home, visually pull it out by filling this missing area with a courtyard type planting. This "new" pulled-forward entrance can be accentuated with an arbor, arch, gate a pair of statues on either side, or similar plantings. (See diagram below.)

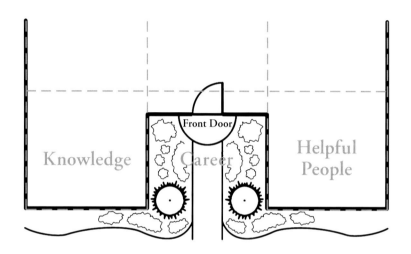

Pulled Forward Entrance

KNOWLEDGE

This is the third bagua area your entrance could be located in if your front door is situated to the left side of your home. The Knowledge gua represents self-cultivation, knowing the most that we can about ourselves. In my Knowledge area I have placed a small reflecting pool with a bench and Japanese lantern nearby. It reminds me to take time to slow down to look at myself, and my life, in the present moment.

Statuary or garden art that reflect your inner nature are also appropriate placements here. Planting something you would like to study and learn more about, such as medicinal herbs, is also an idea; so is creating an area, or garden room, for prayer and contemplation.

A friend of mine has the perfect knowledge room in her garden. She lives on an old dairy farm, and several mature lilacs in this area of her garden have joined together to create a natural arbor, which, once you are inside, feels like a sacred room. She has placed a beautiful gray cement bench in there facing a statue of Mary, and it is the most wonderful place to sit, especially when the lilacs are in bloom. She uses it for meditation and prayer, and also for a cool hiding place after a hot day of gardening.

FAMILY

What I enjoy most in this area of a garden or yard are plants that duplicate themselves often. Hens and chicks, one of my favorites, is an excellent plant visual for family groupings and is perfect here. Also, anything that reseeds itself easily, like Echinacea, will eventually form a nice family stand of one-year, two-year, and older plants. The multiple leaves of ornamental grasses also provide a feeling of group energy here.

Old oaks and towering conifers also provide stately symbols that can link us to the ancestral wisdom of family. Their longevity and stability create feelings of safety and endurance in our lives.

WEALTH

Wealth or abundance gardens, as I call mine, can be fun and full of whimsy. My favorite plant here is the purple-blooming money plant that in the fall has seedpods that resemble paper coins. I also bury actual coins here, and have done a ritual in my own garden with nine Chinese coins. Get creative and come up with your own money adjustment, symbolically planting your own buried treasure so that it may be prolific and grow.

Plants that reseed themselves and give you more for free are wonderful here. I also plant a lot of purple and blue-blooming flowers and trees with round coin shaped leaves, like aspen. This is the ideal place to plant that expensive rare species of peony or place that fabulous piece of garden art you bought at the art fair.

Water, a symbol for the flow of money into our lives, is also welcome here.

Just make sure the pond or fountain is directing that flow of money back towards the house, instead of away from it. Outdoor lighting, shining back onto the house can have the same effect.

FAME

Fame is an area wherein it is important to feel supported. Having tall trees, fencing, or trellis here gives the feng shui sense of having a stable mountain at your back. There are several tall pine trees along the back of my fame and reputation garden. Because there is still a slope here, I have also planted several shrubs that bloom in red to contain the Chi and to keep me from feeling drained. Red weigelia, red phlox, and red bee balm (*Monarda*) help to fill in this garden.

I also have a special burning bush (*Euonymus*) here that was transplanted from the home of a friend. It was quite a challenge to move this large shrub, but with a strong will and determination we did. Because we had to prune it back so severely and cut the root ball to half its size in order to transport it, I thought it might not make it. Yet it did, and grew amazingly well that first season in my yard! To me it holds that same feeling of determination and perseverance in the fame area of my life. In the fall when I am rewarded by its bright red leaves, I see the fruits of my labor made manifest. Remember, fame is about illumination, so any type of lighting here is also auspicious.

CHINESE FIVE ELEMENTS

The Chinese five elements are another feng shui system that you can apply to your garden. Certain areas of the bagua, as you saw on the Bagua Map, also have a natural element associated with them. The main element areas, which form the shape of a cross, are water in Career, wood in Family, fire in Fame, metal in Children and Creativity, and in the center of that cross, earth in Health.

The five elements each have certain characteristics that help to identify and distinguish them from one another. Studying them in Nature is an excellent way to truly understand them. Shortly before teaching my first weeklong workshop on these feng shui elements, I went on a camping trip to Colorado. Fully immersed in Nature, I appreciated the elemental outdoor classroom in which I found myself.

Wealth	Fame *Fire*	Partnerships
Family *Wood*	Health *Earth*	Children and Creativity *Metal*
Knowledge	Career *Water*	Helpful People

Bagua with Five Element Cross

WATER

Watching the free flow of snowmelt streams as they meandered down the mountainside, I could fully understand why water is symbolized with a freely flowing, meandering shape. Water flowing is symbolic to our life's path and the journeys we take along the way. Sometimes our *Career* moves quickly along that path, other times it seems to slow down to a trickle, yet always we are moving and heading to the deep ocean, that place of still water and peace.

Hiking to deep glacier lakes I could physically see the symbology of using the color black for the water element. Deep pools on a cloudy day look as if their depths go on forever. Black is a Yin receding color, which makes you feel you could easily step into it. I also experienced water's color dramatically when a client had black carpeting throughout her home without other elements in place to balance it. Stepping on it was like walking in a wetland, as though I would sink up to my knees at any moment!

WOOD

Wood, the next element I focused on during my vacation, was constantly surrounding me. The ponderosa pines and quaking aspens fed my Soul with the strength of wood, and during windy mountain storms they showed me the wisdom of being flexible. The color green filled my senses and awakened a knowingness that wood is always reaching to the sky in a state of expansion.

A Yang element, wood is often linked to the pioneer spirit of desiring to be the first to reach unexplored horizons. The shape associated with this element is, not surprisingly, a tall, columnar and tree-like. Anything in the blue-green color tones, and/or has a vertical shape rising upward gives us a conscious symbol of this element.

Wood offers us a feeling of strength and stability, as does the support of our *Family*, friends, and ancestors. Realizing that the size of a tree's root system mirrors the extent of the canopy we see above the ground, that support is incredible! Flowering plants and shrubs are also part of the wood family, in essence miniature versions of their cousins the trees.

FIRE

Sitting around the campfire, singing with my children at night, gave me a beautiful opportunity to study fire. I love watching the red-orange flames lap at the wood and move miraculously on their own accord from one area of the fire pit to the other. Always moving, always changing, this element holds the forceful Yang energy of transformation. A glowing beacon to the world it is our illumination of Spirit, reflecting through our personality, that becomes our *Fame and Reputation*. Like a fire we are always burning, though sometimes this flame burns brightly and other times it is just a flicker. The shape associated with fire is pointed and triangular. Again, like wood, the energy is upward moving and Yang, ready to energize and transform all in its path.

EARTH

Connecting with the element of earth was easy in this beautiful mountain setting, especially while out hiking on the trails. Gazing at the yellow earth tone color of the soil beneath my feet, I could feel the absorbing qualities of earth. There is a stabilizing, grounding energy to it; yet also an energetic lifting of my spirit at the same time. I love sleeping on the ground in a sleeping bag; it is so womb like. Once we tried camping with a borrowed tent camper. Its beds were about 4 feet off the ground. It just wasn't the same experience; I could not sleep at night, because I missed the earth's embrace.

Earth holds the center of a space, the place for *Health* and healing. What radiates out from the center is what fills the entire space. Earth is the only element that has aspects of both Yin and Yang. It is giving and anchoring at the same time. The shapes associated with earth are long and low, and square or rectangular.

METAL

Metal has a compact and condensing essence to it. Rocks, stones, and crystal are all part of the metal element, because they are created during this compacting process. Rocky Mountain National Park is full of the metal element, as depicted daily in the rock ledges and stony trails we were climbing. Metal has a refinement that is lacking in all the other elements. It takes us to the bare bones of what we desire to *Create*. There is a purity of purpose, an integrity of form that is present in all the gemstones and precious metals discovered beneath the earth's surface.

As you probably guessed, metal is a Yin element, with energy moving inward. The shapes associated with metal are round and arching. Heated, metal bends easily to form these shapes, and often soft metals, such as mercury, express themselves as round shapes.

GARDEN ADJUSTMENTS USING THE ELEMENTS

These five elements can be used to create garden adjustments that have specific intentions. Again, as learned in the section on Yin and Yang, what we desire is to have a balanced representation of all of these elements in place. A garden that is all metal (Yin), like an all white rock garden with no plantings, will feel as out of balance as one with only red plastic flowers with no green leaves (Yang) surrounding the house. Remember, Nature provides balance without us even thinking about it. Most plants are already a combination of many elements, like the rose with pale pink blossoms (metal), green stems (wood), and pointy thorns (fire).

The Thai people plant pottery into their beautiful garden designs

CHART OF ELEMENTS

WATER	WOOD	FIRE	EARTH	METAL
Yin	*Yang*	*Yang*	*Yin/Yang*	*Yin*
Reflective Surfaces	*Flowers Floral Patterns*	*Candles Lighting*	*Brick/Adobe Tile*	*Metal Crystal/Rock*
Freeform Shapes	*Columnar Vertical Shapes*	*Triangles Pointed Shapes*	*Squares Rectangles*	*Round shapes Arches*
Water Features	*Trees Plant Material*	*Humans Animals*	*Ceramic/Clay Terra Cotta*	*Metal Sculpture*
Black Dark Colors	*Green Blue*	*Red Orange*	*Yellow Earth tones*	*White/Pastels Silver*

Curving, free flowing structures and shapes, such as the sidewalk or garden path, help to symbolize the flow of water, as does the actual element in a water feature. This can be visualized as a career enhancement, symbolizing an easy path and flow to your life's work.

A portable fireplace or fire pit in the Fame area of your yard can help to illuminate who you are to the rest of the world. It can also be a place to gather with family and friends, creating a reputation for fun times. Garden candles and torches are also strong symbols of fire; add them where you would like more of this element to occur.

Metal additions are easy today because so much beautiful metallic garden art is available now. Choose a piece that has meaning for you and place it in a particular area, like my double birdbath placed in Partnership.

Earth brings grounding to an area, and heavy objects, whether they are made of earthenware or not, bring that energy to a space. I also love the way Thailand gardeners add empty pots and ceramic ware to their gardens as sculpture: these are all earthy additions.

Wood is perhaps the most abundant element present in a garden, as the plants themselves represent it. Be aware of those shady spaces where only dead wood may be found from mulch and dying plant material. An important part of the wood energy is to also have the green and growing symbol of suppleness and upward movement. Incorporating the green color, even in a pot color or garden structure, will enliven those "dead wood" areas.

What you are striving to achieve in each of your gardens is a balance of the Yin and the Yang. These Yin and Yang characteristics can be found in the specific elements you choose for your garden. Be a detective and ask yourself, "Does this garden feel balanced?" If not, do some further sleuthing, using the element chart provided, to identify which elements are present, and which are missing. Adding the element that is missing, or removing portions of one in too much abundance, will bring about the perfectly balanced garden you are looking for.

CHAPTER 5

NATURAL
GARDENING STYLE

Close your eyes and imagine you are a hawk flying high above the surface of the earth. Now look down and notice what shapes capture your attention on the ground. Where are the round, oval and irregular shapes found? Who has created the squares and rectangular shapes in our world? Yes, from this vantage point it is revealing to observe that Nature plants in circles. The canopy of trees, the shapes of lakes, the mountain ranges with tall vertical peaks and deep valleys, and gentle rolling hills, all are organic, round, oval, or irregular in shape. In stark contrast are the views provided by man. The distinct square and rectangular shapes of our homes and office buildings, the square divisions that roads create, even the design of the majority of our farmers' fields; all of these are squares within more squares.

So why does Nature plant in circles? Seeds disperse in a circle radiating out from the parent plant. Plants, shrubs, trees all grow in that same identifying shape reaching upward for the sun. Natural lakes and ponds have curving edges and are circular in shape. Even mud puddles are gently rounded! I'm no scientist, but I believe it has to do with the way molecules, and in turn energy, hold their shape. Clustering around each other, the individual pieces are held

The bumblebee, an important garden pollinator, at work on a thistle plant

together in this form with the least amount of work. I know from my experience working with groups of people, that it is easier to keep them together and to build energy if we are sitting or standing in a circle.

In feng shui we look to our surroundings, analyze where we feel the best, such as a naturally occurring setting, and attempt to recreate that same experience in our gardens. One of the basic beliefs in feng shui is that by imitating and reflecting on the balance found in Nature, we can then create this same harmony in our own lives. If we take our clues from naturally occurring vegetation and waterways, the best shape for a garden is organic and curving, including several round and freeform shapes.

Why then are most gardens designed to follow the square outline of a home, or the straight lines of a sidewalk? As humans we have a tendency to use rigid square shapes in an effort to compartmentalize and bring a sense of control to the garden. We feel safer and more protected with four walls around us. The wildness of nature feels better contained and controlled this way; yet, in this rigidity we loose the free flow of the energy, or Chi, we so cherished in the first place.

Stephan enjoys the circular snowmelt gardens at Glacier National Park in Montana

GARDEN PATTERN AND DESIGN

From my experience in feng shui centered landscape and garden design, I have seen some specific planting patterns that have intuitively emerged. The most important garden spaces for generating Chi flow are those that immediately surround the home. Creating gardens that encircle the house on all sides, sets up a template from which this energy can flow. This hugging of the home with the bright colors of flowers and vibrant green growing plants encircles the house with an aura of life force. The feng shui advantage of this arrangement is that it provides an abundant supply of Chi to enter interior spaces, as well. Once that life force is inside, it is a benefit to all who live there. As you work in your garden or share it with family and friends during garden tours, you walk completely around your home, and this physical movement also generates and nourishes the Chi flow.

The second layer that seems to emerge in the garden's architecture is an outer ring of garden, usually located on the outside boundary of the yard. In a rural setting, it may be where the edge of the lawn moves into the wildness of the woods. In the city, it is the outer boundary of the property, usually along the fence line. This design creates the outer walls of the container I call garden space.

In between these two edges or boundaries is a green area filled with lawn, walking paths, or patio areas. This space is essential to living with, and the enjoyment of, a garden. It offers a means of movement from one garden to the next, and also space to play, entertain, relax and just be enclosed by the gardens, basking in their beauty and privacy.

The house becomes the center of the garden space, with concentric rings of garden surrounding it like ripples in a pond. Energy flows in and out of this arrangement easily, circling the home and also spiraling in and out of the center to the gardens; and back, house to gardens, gardens to house. This design creates beautiful gardens that have a solid sense of boundary, becoming a vibrant container for healthy garden Chi.

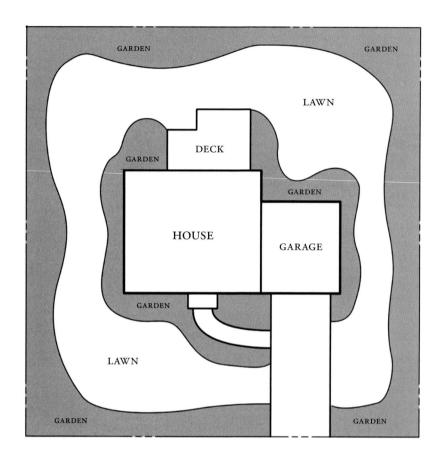

GARDENING WITH NATURE

I started gardening organically over 20 years ago. I find it very interesting that this coincides with the beginning of my spiritual journey into balance with myself and those around me. That was when I first realized how intricately everything in our world is related, and that the chemicals I put on my garden do make a difference in this world. By choosing natural pest control over the often more efficient chemical, store-bought ones, I have left openings in my garden for butterflies and other beneficial insects to live. Choosing organic fertilizers helps me to be a better steward of the ground water that feeds my neighbor's and my wells. Letting a tree decay naturally in the forest helps to feed Mother Nature's cycle of death and rebirth, providing shelter for bugs and rodents and food for fungi. What we do as individuals does have a profound effect on all of us. I choose for that effect to be a less invasive, positive one by following methods that garden *with* Nature instead of against her.

SOIL PREPARATION

Spending time and money improving your soil pays back immensely in the long run. When we first moved into our log home, there was little here but sandy loam. The previous owners had done some typical landscaping out the front door with junipers and hostas, yet the remaining three sides of the house felt neglected and barren. It was literally just sand with small patches of weeds and construction debris tossed here and there. Lucky for me I saw this as a "blank canvas" opportunity for me to design the feng shui gardens of my dreams.

The first item I received as a birthday present from my dad that same summer was 50 yards of topsoil; something only a true gardener would be happy and excited about. This was still not nearly enough for the lawn and landscaping I had envisioned. So slowly, over the years, I continue to amend the soil every chance I get. Because of the sandy loam here, adding sphagnum peat moss is the best way to improve its water retention capabilities. My next favorite soil builder is composted cow manure, because it adds a nice balance of organic matter and a full range of trace elements. What is amazing is it has no smell, just a wonderful earthy look and feel.

Rotted leaves from the woods add the necessary microorganisms, the tiny almost invisible creepy crawlies that make the whole decomposition, soil building process happen. These guys can also be added by composting your kitchen scraps together with leaves and yard debris. Composting is fun and easy, and we will discuss various methods in a later section.

It makes sense to provide the most hospitable growing environment for your plants that you can. There is nothing worse than spending a lot of money on a "dream plant" (you know, the one whose photo you drool over in the catalog and envision growing exuberantly in your garden), and then watch it struggle and die because the soil could not support its basic needs. It took me a while to figure out there is a scientific way to measure these needs and have them fulfilled. It is called a soil test, and is very easy to do yourself.

Once a year, I would deliver a soil sample from a mix of the soils in my gardens to the Michigan State University agricultural extension office downtown. Three weeks later, by mail, they would tell me what basic nutrients my soil was lacking; but that was never enough information for me. I wanted to know exactly which gardens were lacking what, and to know a month later if I had added enough of the recommended nutrients to correct the situation. I could have the extension office do numerous tests for me at different times of the year, but this is too much leg work and waiting for me. The answer, and my best discovery, has been the do-it-yourself soil test kits found at the garden center. They come with 10–20 test strips and make you feel like a kid in chemistry class. The procedure is very easy; you mix soil from a single area with distilled water, shake it in the bottle provided, and then insert a test strip to see what colors show up on it. These colors are then compared to a color chart in the kit that tells you what level your soil's pH is.

pH represents the measurement of Hydrogen-Ion concentration in the soil, telling you if your soil is considered acidic or alkaline. Number assignments are given, ranging between 0 and 14, to indicate where the soil pH would fall on a simple color-coded acidic-basic scale. A pH number of 7 is neutral, while any number below 7 is considered acidic, and above 7 is alkaline or basic. Monitoring pH levels is important, because it determines how well plants are able to use the available nutrients in the soil.

What I love about a home kit is the flexibility of being able to do several tests from different areas in the garden. For instance, my Abundance Garden has a lot of acid-loving plants in it, like rhododendrons and hydrangeas. These plants prefer a more acidic, lower pH level than the normal reading of 6.5. I can test this level in that particular garden and make the necessary adjustments if the pH is too high. Likewise, the vegetable garden likes a higher pH reading, about 7 or 8 for optimum growth, so I can test if this needs to be corrected. Adjusting pH can take a long time, so be patient in this process (although raising it is usually much easier than lowering it).

To increase the pH level of your soil (increase alkalinity) add:
- *Lime*
- *Ground limestone*
- *Oyster shells*

To lower the pH of your soil (increase acidity) add:
- *Organic matter*
- *Compost*
- *Manure*

Another important test included in the kit measures the amount of nitrogen, phosphorus, and potassium that is present in the soil. These are the elements usually added to our gardens as fertilizers. Instead of waiting for symptoms on the plants to tell you what they need, it is helpful to be proactive. Usually when the plant has turned yellow, it is too late in the growing season to save. Most organic fertilizers need time to break down into the soil; they do not magically shift the soil's condition overnight.

Fertilizers can be classified into two different types: natural or synthetic. Natural fertilizers, derived from Nature, are either organic or inorganic. True organic fertilizers come from plant and animal wastes and are carbon based. They are slow acting and non-burning and do not harm the microorganisms within the soil; in fact, they actually feed them. Inorganic fertilizers are non-carbon based, naturally occurring chemicals, such as limestone, rock phosphate, or sulfate of potash. These *can* burn plants if over applied.

Synthetic fertilizers are "man made", and their common nitrogen sources such as ammonia, ammonium sulfate, and urea, are by-products from the oil and natural gas industry. These fertilizers, if over applied, have a tendency to burn plants, and often leach into our ground water through surface runoff caused by rain or over watering. This runoff creates an algae bloom imbalance in our lakes and streams, increasing the mortality rate of fish and aquatic life. Synthetic fertilizers also do not provide food for the important microorganisms found in soil, and over time these essential organisms will die. The soil then loses aeration and texture, turning into a hard and lifeless structure.

Organic gardener Penny Kelly, the author of *From the Soil to the Stomach*, says plants fed synthetic fertilizers are like "kids on a sugar high." Causing rapid growth and absorption, these fertilizers ultimately stress the plant, as it becomes a chemical junkie, waiting for the next "quick high." Organic fertilizers provide a steadier flow of elements to the soil, slowly breaking down over time. There is no threat of fertilizer burn to the plants, and they do not contaminate our precious ground water.

As mentioned before, the soil test kit will measure the three most important elements needed in your soil for healthy plant production. These three important elements are nitrogen, phosphorus, and potassium, often symbolized as initials N, P, and K. There are several trace elements necessary as well, and most of these will be supplied by the organic amendments you will make.

NITROGEN

Nitrogen is important for growth because it promotes lush green foliage. That is why it is used so extensively on healthy lawns. Leafy vegetables, like spinach and lettuce, also benefit from high levels of this element. My first soil test revealed very low levels of nitrogen in my soil, probably due to its sandy content. By increasing this one element, I noticed a dramatic increase in plant size, almost to the point of doubling the height and width of what had been there the year before!

Because it is easily washed away by rainwater, the nitrogen level in your soil can deplete rapidly. For this reason it is especially important to test for and add nitrogen regularly. Add more nitrogen organically to your soil with the following:

- *Dried blood*
- *Fish meal*
- *Ground hoof and horn*
- *Bone meal*
- *Cottonseed meal*

PHOSPHORUS

Phosphorus is essential for strong root formation and development. This, in turn, makes for sturdier and denser stem growth. It also protects the plant against disease and stress from poor weather conditions. Add phosphorus to your soil with the addition of:

- *Bone meal*
- *Bat guano combined with compost*
- *Colloidal rock phosphate*
- *Soft rock phosphate*

POTASSIUM

Potassium is the element found in soil that helps to support a plant's ability to set flowers, fruits, or vegetables. Increasing the potassium level in my garden has yielded more flowers and a longer range of bloom time. It is also responsible for sugar formation in fruits and vegetables, making for better tasting produce. Add potassium to your soil with the following:

- *Rock potash*
- *Greensand*
- *Seaweed meal*
- *Wood ashes*
- *Cow manure*

TRACE ELEMENTS

Healthy plants need over sixteen essential nutrients for optimum growth. Although nitrogen, phosphorus, and potassium are the three most important, and the ones a home soil test will measure, the other thirteen, called "trace elements," are necessary on a smaller scale. Copper, magnesium, iron, salt, and calcium are a few of these elements that are needed in only very small amounts. Applying liquid seaweed and or liquid animal manure, as well as compost, can adequately provide these elements.

MANURE OR COMPOST "TEA"

Making your own liquid manure or compost tea is easy. Gather a large plastic bucket, water, a large piece of cotton burlap cloth (or a natural fabric bag like an old cotton pillowcase), and some animal manure or ripe compost. For the manure, sheep is best, but cow, pig, goat, or horse manure can be used. Wrap the manure or compost up in the burlap cloth or bag and tie securely, like a giant tea bag. Let it float in the bucket of water, or suspend it from a stake across the top of the bucket, overnight or for several days until the water is a rich brown color. Remove the bag and leave the bucket covered. You can use this straight on the garden, provided the soil has been watered down first. It also makes an excellent foliar spray.

COMPOSTING

The addition of compost is essential to a healthy natural garden. It is the ideal way to return as much organic matter as possible back to the soil. This is the same cycle nature uses to nourish itself. For example, a tree, in essence, is a self-feeding organism. It drops a plethora of leaves at its base line, which in turn rot and decay, feeding its roots. What a great set up!

Decomposing vegetation provides a home and food for millions of soil organisms and microorganisms. These organisms break down waste into the valuable elements and trace minerals plants need. Anything organic in Nature can be placed on the compost pile: fruit and vegetable scraps, eggshells, coffee grounds, grass clippings, and leaves. What *does not* work well here are meat products, processed foods like bread or pasta, diseased plant material, and anything with seeds you would not like more of.

People often ask me if animals get into my compost pile, or does it smell? My compost bin is constructed very roughly of a simple wood frame surrounded by square wire fencing material, which keeps the dog and critters out and the compost in. I also cover the top layer with a few inches of soil, which helps hide the smell and also speed up the decomposition process. It is placed in a hidden area beside the garage, and I have not had any problems with wild animals or smells. However, contained compost stations are difficult to turn,

A simple compost bin made of wooden stakes and square wire fencing

and to be honest; I rarely do it. It still makes compost; it just takes a few years. I have also been experimenting with a new and easier way of composting. These experiments have led me to what I call "direct composting," which involves placing the compost right in the bed where it will be used. This process works best as a way to build soil in annual or vegetable beds that are empty during late fall and winter. My family just piles the fruit and veggie scraps in these designated areas, again covering with soil when the ground isn't frozen. If it is available, I may even use snow, although the heat from the decaying matter gets warm, even in the winter, and melts holes in the drifts. In the spring I dig this half-decomposed mush into the ground to condition the soil. This method saves having to turn the compost pile, and also transporting it again to the desired location.

I also direct compost into new beds I am designing. Digging up an area to fill in the following season, it becomes the compost spot of choice. I am always amazed how quickly the microbes do their job. I have seen melon rinds break down in two weeks in the summer!

What is important to remember when composting is you that need equal parts of green and brown organic material. Just kitchen waste in a compost bin will become high in ammonia and smell awful! A bin full of only dried leaves and twigs will take a much longer time to decompose without the green material present.

I have heard stories of grandmothers digging in a melon rind with every new plant, or burying banana peels next to rose bushes to provide potassium. I have experimented with both melon and banana peels with great results. Our ancestors were wise people and master gardeners, too!

What I like best about composting is that it keeps a lot of stinky garbage from ending up in landfills, rotting away in plastic bags, and puts it to good use. It connects us back to the primitive cycles of death and rebirth. Out of ashes and decay new life is created.

NATURE AS MASTER COMPOSER

When we first moved to the woods over 16 years ago I have to admit I still had a "city mind." I was accustomed to trees and shrubs being neatly trimmed, dead branches removed, and fall leaves raked and picked up at the curb. That first year in our new woodland home, when a tree died in the woods, my husband would dutifully cut it down and neatly stack it into a pile in the woods. My son Stephan, an avid bird and animal lover, opened our eyes to this folly. He said Nature just lets a tree fall where it may, and then lets the bugs and animals use it for a home and food as it slowly decays on the forest floor. Nature is not concerned with how "tidy" the woods are. Fallen logs are part of the natural decomposition process of a forest.

Since then, we leave trees where they fall, unless they are across the driveway, the woodland paths, or in the gardens. We also do not cut down any dead trees, unless they could harm humans or structures if they fell. These dead trees create natural habitats, which become homes for insects, birds, and wildlife. This act has rewarded us with an increase of woodpeckers seen at our home, especially the rare pileated woodpecker. This bird chisels huge three to five inch chunks of wood from these dead trees searching for insects.

Hardy Hibiscus, "Kopper King"

GARDEN VISITORS

Bees, slugs, dragonflies, ladybugs, aphids, moles, and their friends are all under the heading I like to call "garden visitors". Some of these visitors are more welcome than others. When we are gardening in partnership with Nature Spirits, discrimination between good guests and bad isn't done. They all have a right to be here, because they are all a part of Nature. This concept is still challenging for me on some days, especially when the Japanese beetles have taken up permanent dining residence in the beautiful rose-colored hibiscus flowers I have waited patiently to see bloom.

There have been studies that indicate a plant's energy vibration determines how attractive they are to insects. Those with higher vibrational fields tend to become "invisible," while those with problems seem to put out an "all you can eat" sign. Healthy plants radiate a particular complex of electromagnetic signals

that are different from the signals given off by unhealthy plants. Insects and pests pick up on these alterations, using their antenna as built-in radar, then find the weaker plant and attack it. Even when healthy and unhealthy plants are placed next to each other, and their stems and leaves were intertwined, the insects ignore the healthy leaves and that plant remains intact!

This makes sense with the survival-of-the-fittest theories. Those plants with a higher vibration are left untouched and can continue growing to create a stronger seed for next year's crop. This leaves the underachievers behind to become necessary food for the insects that are all part of the intricate balance to life, and still important, be they only a slug. And that slug may be dinner for the blue jay, which is a meal for the hawk, and so on.

Michelle Small Wright, owner of Perelandra Gardens, a co-creative research garden, does nothing to interfere with the insect populations on her plants there. She believes, "The insects move in and out, creating an intricate pattern that seems to magically weave into the larger fabric of the garden whole." She views their sudden appearance as the Nature kingdom's way of drawing our attention to a particular plant and its situation. This goes along with the idea that the plant is in need of something to help raise its vibration. We can then focus in on what that individual plant needs and provide it.

I have noticed that on occasion the so-called insect pests in my garden have been helpful in a roundabout way. Every spring the green-lined bugs attack my chrysanthemums, leaving behind unsightly patterns of tiny brown dots on the leaves. I proceed to pinch off the tops of each plant about two to three inches. Amazingly, this just happens to correspond with the exact time the gardening books advise me to top off the mums for more vigorous bushy bloom in the fall. By September the chrysanthemums have branched out with beautiful blossoms on sturdy stems that do not need staking, and the green-lined bugs are nowhere to be seen.

Desiring to work in a co-creative manner with these less-than-desirable insects, I am still not to the lofty place of allowing them to eat what they will. Because I am still in the process of building my soil and, in turn, the plant's vitality, I often resort to less than honorable solutions to control the insects.

My number-one choice is the ruthless seek-and-squeeze mission with my bare hands. I know this sounds murderous, but they do receive warnings before I come to squish. I adamantly encourage them to relocate to the woods to eat what they will, but in my garden there are boundaries to adhere to. Those caught trespassing may pay the consequences.

My second method of control is soapy garlic water in an 8-ounce spray bottle. Let the garlic steep in the bottle filled with warm water overnight. In the morning remove the garlic, add a squeeze of liquid dish soap, shake well, and spray on the parts of any plant you want left alone. Be sure to spray the undersides of the leaves, too, as this is their favorite hiding place. This method works fine until it rains, or you wash it off with the hose. It then must be re-applied to be effective.

The biggest deterrent to pests that I have found is your diligence and your energy in the garden. Just touching the plants and being around them seems to put up an invisible shield that keeps most pests away. That is why when we leave for vacation the pests suddenly move in. Your energy is no longer felt, and the walls of protection come down.

Even with a lofty vision of Nature's balance, sometimes it helps to add some allies to the garden mix. Beneficial insects can provide a great benefit here. The easiest way to introduce beneficial helpers to the garden is to entice the ones in your own neighborhood with their favorite foods. Most of these types of insects love flowering herbs and plants high in pollen and sweet nectar. That translates to sweet-smelling flowers that create an inviting habitat for them, and are beautiful for you. Insects also require some type of water source, as simple as a shallow dish filled with pebbles, or as elaborate as an extensive water garden. They will also need shelter, which is easily provided by rock borders, perennial plants, and shrubs.

Garden pests thrive in a monoculture garden. That is why farmers, with their acres of corn or soybeans, can have difficulties with unbalanced insect populations. The more diverse the plant life in your garden, the less likely a specific pest will be able to establish itself. This also increases the chances of providing a home for the very insect that will help keep a pest in balance.

BENEFICIAL INSECT GROUPS

The four types of beneficial insect groups are predators, parasitoids, pollinators, and soil builders. All help the garden in their own unique way. These four types are described below, followed by a section on my favorite insect "friends." I'm sure you will recognize many of them.

PREDATORS

These groups of insects, such as praying mantids, have voracious appetites, do not discriminate, and devour anything that moves in their path. Some, such as the ladybird beetle (ladybug), have developed a taste for more specific prey, like aphids.

PARASITOIDS

Parasitoids, as their name hints to, derive nourishment from the body of a host insect. They do not kill the host immediately: instead they lay their eggs on, in or nearby it. Trichogramma wasps are part of this group. When their eggs hatch, hundreds of hungry babies can then take care of all the unwanted visitors on one infested plant. These parasites usually have very specific hosts. They are the most efficient of the beneficial insects, because they are able to fight off detrimental pests without endangering the lives of other good bugs.

POLLINATORS

Although they do not eat harmful insects, they provide a valuable service to the garden as a whole. Without their constant travel from flower to flower most plants would be unable to reproduce and make seeds for the following season.

SOIL BUILDERS

These creatures, mainly the earthworm family, help to aerate the soil, eat decaying plant matter, and leave behind valuable natural fertilizer in their castings.

MINNIE'S FAVORITE BENEFICIAL INSECTS

Below is a list of some of my favorite insect "friends" and how to attract them. Often we see them flying around our plants, but don't even know or appreciate the important role they play in the intricate balance of a healthy garden.

DAMSELFLIES AND DRAGONFLIES

These beauties are good predators of aphids, flies, and mosquitoes. They need a body of water close by, such as a fish pod or water garden. The aquatic nymphs of both these insects love mosquito larvae.

PRAYING MANTIDS

Also known as praying mantis, these striking insects tend to eat any other insect in sight. Several years ago I purchased three mantid egg cases and tied them to the lower rung of my rose arch in the garden. One morning, looking out the kitchen window, I saw a mass of insects crawling up the arch. That mass was hundreds of tiny praying mantis babies marching single file to the very tip of the metal structure. They were all congregating at the top, unsure about where to head next. I carefully scooped off a group at a time and moved them to known aphid-infected plants. They did a wonderful job that year of keeping the garden pest free, and late in the season I spotted two or three full adult-size "pets" still in the garden. They had favorite plants to hang out in, and the kids and I named them and played a game of hide-and-seek looking for them. When we are lucky they gift us with their offspring the following year.

Praying mantid: garden pet and predator

LACEWINGS

These fairy-like insects are attracted to the pollen of sunflowers. Their larvae are extremely voracious predators and have a good reputation for sticking around the garden. These nocturnal insects eat aphids, mealy bugs, nymphs of scale insects, and other soft-bodied insects.

LADYBIRD BEETLES

The insects can be purchased from garden catalogues, and when my lively bunch arrived, the instructions said to place them in the refrigerator or immediately in the garden. Also called ladybugs, they have a reputation for flying away from the garden after you purchase them. To encourage them to stay, dampen plants before releasing them, release just before sunrise or at sun-down (cooler time of day), and gently lay handfuls at the base of aphid-infected plants. Do not scatter them about. Encourage them to stay by planting tansy, angelica, and scented geraniums.

BUMBLEBEES

These chubby and more docile bees gather pollen on their hairy bodies and legs and are super-efficient cross-pollinators. They love coreopsis, lavender, and butterfly bush. Bumblebees often nest in the ground during the growing season. To avoid digging into their nests unknowingly, watch carefully for a string of bees entering a small hole in the ground in your flowerbeds. Leave at least a three-foot diameter 'no dig' zone around this hole for your safety. The good news is only the queen and a few of her helpers survive the winter, and they rarely take up residence in last year's holes.

HONEYBEES

This amazing species is largely responsible for pollinating most of the flowers, fruits, and vegetables in your garden. They are especially attracted to white sage and other flowering herbs. Honey bees only sting to defend their home, or as a last defense. When they are disturbed away from the hive they would rather flee than use their stinger because doing so is suicide. Respect them and they will respect you. You may want to consider leaving that dead tree near your garden alone, as it may bless you by providing a home for a wondrous colony of honeybees!

TRICHOGRAMMA WASPS

These wasps have tiny stout bodies, and are one of the smallest insects on the planet, the size of some bacteria. Don't worry about being stung by one; you will be lucky if you ever see one. You can easily purchase a strain that enjoys your particular climate through garden mail order catalogs. Trichogramma wasps are so small because they are parasitoids of other insect's eggs, including fruit worm, hornworm, loppers, and cabbageworms. Their advantage is they stop infestations from these pests before they are even born.

SPIDERS

Spiders get such a bad rap in our society because their benefits are not well known. According to the Doar and Olkowski article *Common Sense Pest Control*, "The Chinese report that arachnids are responsible for about 80% of the biological control in a garden. Spiders are among the most important predators of insects, and their role in controlling insect pests is often underappreciated by humans." They are very busy insects in the garden; but again, you can set boundaries with the Spider Deva about not having them hunt inside the house. One friend agreement is they can live in her basement as long as she never sees them.

EARTHWORMS

Earthworms can eat their weight in decaying matter each day. They can also live for an amazing 10–12 years! Their casting (earthworm poop) is like gold because it is high in all three major elements the soil needs: phosphorus, nitrogen and potassium. They also aerate the soil and are a most welcome addition. Adding organic matter to the soil, such as decaying leaves and compost, will bring them crawling to your garden.

When digging in the garden, take care to look out for them. I treat them like royalty; finding a safe plant to relocate them to. Despite popular childhood beliefs, they cannot survive being cut in two.

COMPANION PLANTING

There are also companion plants that can act as natural repellants in your garden. Because of strong, disagreeable odors or a bitter taste, they often discourage insects from coming anywhere near them or other plants growing nearby. Interplanting marigolds, chives, onions, garlic, or rue among more vulnerable plants, such as dahlia or rose, can create a natural defense against insect pests. Aromatic plants – such as tansy, nasturtiums, yarrow, savory, and thyme – scattered throughout the garden are also great deterrents.

UNINVITED GUESTS

Our gardens also attract the "four-leggeds" from Nature, and sometimes in their quest for survival they inadvertently cause damage to the gardens. The questions I am most often asked are about keeping destructive animals out of the garden. Again, wanting to work co-creatively with them, my first choice is to establish an active communication. Remember, they were here before us, yet we as humans tend to brazenly come in and take over, claiming ownership of the land for ourselves.

Earlier, I spoke of an Overlighting Deva for individual animal species, such as the Deva of the moles. Going into meditation to connect to this Deva is a first step toward finding out why they are there and how you can work together.

Moles are creatures I have conversations with throughout the growing season. I know they are not eating my plants, but larvae and grubs in the lawn, preferably those which will emerge and cause havoc later on. Moles can be an indication that there is an imbalance happening under the soil, such as an increase in Japanese beetle larvae.

Despite this, they do cause some nasty tunnels and holes in the yard, which can be a nuisance to trip over. At other times they displace a plant's roots from contact with the soil, and it may die. This is what was happening in my garden, and why I first chose to contact the Overlighting Mole Deva.

Sitting in meditation outside, right near a newly dug tunnel, I asked to speak to the big guy in charge of mole activity in my yard. A sweet brown face full of fur with no eyes slowly appeared in my vision. Somewhat dazed, like I had just woken him up, he asked what the problem was. After I explained my dilemma, he asked me where I would like him to go to find his supper. I told him he could go anywhere else on the twelve acres besides the gardens that I cultivate near the house. He said they could do that, but what would I do for them? We came to an agreement that if they relocated, any of their tunnels found in the woods were to be left in peace. This would be my way of honoring them in the wild and understanding they still needed a place to be. Conversely, if I found tunnels in my gardens, I had permission to step on them to remind the moles they were getting too close. So after that, any tunnels my family or I see in the woods, especially across the trails, are consciously avoided or walked over. Often I am taking newcomers for walks in the woods and say, "Mole tunnel, please step over."

This dramatically decreased the amount of tunneling that was happening in my garden area. It is interesting that sometimes they tunnel in the sandy driveway, but stop short just before the vegetable garden or flower garden. Whenever I see the moles' tunnels in the woods, I am reminded of our agreement and the relationship that we have.

My most important realization from these conversations is that the animal is only trying to survive, just like us. Asking it to leave without thinking where it may relocate to is selfish on our part. I know living in the woods makes it easier to find them new homes, yet often in cities there is a small woodlot or park nearby where you can send them. They may even enjoy moving to a wild corner of your own yard.

A few years ago my garden friend living in the city had some trouble with yellow jackets nesting in her perennial beds. Every time she dug in that garden their nest was disturbed, and she was in danger of being stung. Looking for a new home for them was challenging, for if we sent them to a neighbor's yard, there was a good chance the nest would be sprayed with a pesticide. She finally remembered a nearby woodlot, about a block away, and asked them to relocate there. It took a few conversations to convince them, but they finally left and have never returned.

What I find just as fascinating as talking with Animal Devas is figuring out why these animals have suddenly turned up so boldly in my life. There is surely a message I am to learn from them. Ted Andrews' book, *Animal Speak*, is the manual I use to help me figure that out. Ted says, "A study of Nature Totems is essential for understanding how the spiritual is manifesting within our natural life." The stronger our connection to Nature, the more often these messages will appear, providing us with awareness about a situation.

For instance, the deer may be showing up in your garden to eat the new shoots of your azalea, but also to teach you lessons in being gentle and kind. Perhaps, as Andrews writes, it is "time to be more gentle with yourself or with others in your life. Is there something you are trying to force in your life? Are you being too critical and uncaring of yourself?" These are important questions to ask when desiring to reach deeper into the hidden meaning of encounters with deer. Likewise, any animal you have an interaction with will always have some type of message for you, if you are willing to listen.

My second best means of critter balancing in the garden are my dog and cat. Mishka, our beautiful Samoyed, keeps the deer, rabbit, and even wild turkey, at bay. Her regular patrols of the yard keep her scent ever present and mark the human's territory. She even likes to think she controls what birds may fly in her "air space" above the house, including those large noisy ones called airplanes. Tao, the Siamese cat, does her part with the rodent population, especially the mice in the garage. Sometimes I think they are mere play toys to her, something to amuse her on a warm summer day. She doesn't take her critter control job quite as seriously as Mishka.

OTHER GARDEN ALLIES

There are several beneficial animal friends, besides our pets, that are helpful to a garden's growth. Birds, bats, toads, frogs, fish, and salamanders all eat a large variety of insects that would otherwise be munching on our flowers.

The first food of choice for many birds, including chickadees, house wrens, towhees and phoebes, are insects, followed by seeds and fruit only when that

supply dwindles. In summer, a chickadee eats from 200–500 insects a day! Baby birds hatching in the spring keep their parents busy supplying them with food as they can increase in size by ⅓ to ½ daily! What better way to eliminate those newly hatched aphids or cutworms?

Encouraging birds to stay on your property year round is well worth the effort. Provide them with the basic provisions of food, protection, and water, and they will enhance your gardens with their presence. Thick shrubs like elderberry and honeysuckle make great nesting and perching areas. As do climbing plants like virginia creeper and wild grape. They also love trees such as flowering crab, balsam fir, birch, red cedar, and fruit trees. Feeding birds a combination of suet and seed in the winter helps to satisfy the needs of many different species.

Every winter we place a small real evergreen tree on our deck. It is called the "birdfeeder tree" and from it we hang pinecones filled with peanut butter, corncobs, strands of millet, and any old stale bread products from the kitchen. We also string cranberries and peanuts in the shell. The bluejays love to shell the peanuts and it keeps them busy and out of the birdfeeders, the same goes for the squirrels. It is our give- away tree, and situated right next to the dining table it provides hours of entertainment on a snowy day.

Provide water in shallow bird baths no more than 3" deep. Having a rough edge and interior surface helps them to perch easily. Place your birdbath high enough so it is away from the danger of cats, and in an open area where the approach of enemies can be seen. It is important to clean them often to keep them free of algae growth. In the winter months, a simple electric heating device in the water keeps this supply open year round. In the winter pond I lay branching twigs over the ice to allow for perching for the smaller birds and easier access to the open water.

Bats, though often misunderstood, are the champions of mosquito control, and that is an important feat here in Michigan where the mosquito has been named the "State Insect". They can eat over 1,000 of these bothersome outdoor pests in an hour! We welcome bats to our garden with a bat house situated high in a tree away from the house. They are fun to watch from the deck circling the sky at dusk.

Fish, toads, frogs, and salamanders are some of the most welcome residents in my garden. People are amazed I do not feed the fish during the summer. They receive all their nourishment from the mosquito larvae and other water bugs they find in the water. In the winter their body metabolisms slow down and they do not eat. Only if we have an unusually warm day and I see that they are active do I feed them a dash of fish food. They often look at it like foreign material, until eventually one of them gingerly tries it. I'm sure it is a far cry in texture and taste from what they are used to eating.

The first year I had a pond, I carefully caught all the fish in the fall and put them indoors in aquariums. They were huge! It is amazing how quickly a five-cent feeder goldfish can grow in one season. After losing several fish each winter to indoor aquarium diseases, I learned they fare much better if left in their outdoor environment.

The frogs also stop eating and hibernate in the winter. They dig themselves into the pots of water plants that I move to the deep end of the pond each fall. It is said they actually have a type of anti-freeze in their blood that lets them almost freeze yet not die. That seems to be the case, because every year we have a healthy number of frogs overwinter. The count one summer was sixteen!

What is most important for the hibernation process of frogs and fish is that the pond does not freeze over completely, another reason to invest in an electric heater. Decaying plant material can build up toxic gasses under the ice that can potentially kill them. It is advisable to remove all dead and dying stems and leaves from the pond before winter progresses. This also makes clean up easier in the spring.

Toads and salamanders are night-visiting amphibians that also do insect patrol for our gardens. The american toad (*Bufo americanus*) is the most common in the United States and grows 3–5 inches in size. Toads eat four times the capacity of their stomachs in a 24-hour period. They also have a strong

We had a frog count of sixteen in the pond one year

homing instinct, often taking up residence in the same garden for several years. Salamanders are happiest in moist and dark environments. They generally feed at night on grubs, sow bugs, snails, and some spiders. Stephan often finds them hiding under log piles in the shade of the woods. They are beautiful and often associated with wood nymphs and the fairy realm.

So you see, with all these natural aids for insect infestations, there is a balanced plan already in place. Nature is designed to keep herself in a perfect state of equilibrium. It is only when we humans create a break in the cycle, such as those caused by the use of pesticides, that this stability is threatened.

CHAPTER 6

MEDICINAL HERBS

What I learned closest to home was what
was ultimately of the greatest value.

Henry David Thoreau

⚘

Did you know there is potentially a free pharmacy of medicine right outside your front door? Since being a part of a medicinal study group I have learned to identify and use these amazing plants for my family's health and for myself.

In 1996, a group of four friends came together with a love for herbs, flowers, and Mother Earth. We called our monthly gathering time "First Friday Friends of Herbs" and soon our membership grew. Our shared interests spurred a continued study of herbs and the soon to be discovered "beneficial weeds", that we were at that time tossing from our gardens.

My gardens have always included a vegetable patch and some culinary herbs for flavoring, yet this was the first time I truly looked to the plants as medicine for healing. It has been an eye-opening experience and one that has further strengthened my connection to these plants. I love the empowering

Purple pansies have such
cheery faces and are also
colorful salad additions

feeling of knowing what you need to care for yourself is already growing nearby. Like a pioneer foraging off the land, I no longer have to run to the drugstore every time someone gets sick. I also save myself a lot of money on teas and lotions, and over the counter medications.

HERBAL GATHERING AND STORING

How many of us grew up afraid to eat anything from the wild? And with the use of commercial chemicals being applied so ignorantly to the earth, it *is* frightening in some places. But, in your own natural organic garden, nearby woodland, or organically fertilized pesticide-free lawn, there is a plethora of edibles to enjoy!

What is most important when you decide you want to gather your own plants for medicine is correct plant identification. I suggest you spend an entire year in relationship with one particular species of plant to fully understand it; watching it throughout a cycle of seasons, learning its growth habits, studying its leaf, flower and seed characteristics. Purchase a good plant identification guide; or better yet, have someone already extremely familiar with the plant help you correctly identify it.

Sketching and meditating with a plant is also a wonderful way to become familiar with it and the energy or medicine it provides. This is what we did in the Friends of Herbs group, only we chose one plant per month to focus on. We then learned how to make teas, and tinctures, and salves with that plant.

Once you have made a positive identification and started building a relationship with a specific plant species, you are ready to begin gathering it to use. The highest energy and medicine is found in live plant material. This form is always my first choice when using it for healing.

Yet sometimes we need a larger supply than what is growing at that time or we would rather not create gaping holes in the garden. Also, here in Michigan in the winter, our gardens are sleeping for almost six months out of the year. This is why drying herbs for later use is wise.

This process is very easy; the hardest part is remembering to do it. I am usually very diligent about gathering herbs in the fall, once I realize my fresh supply will soon be covered in snow. What is challenging is reaping the bounty of my herbs throughout the *entire* growing season, and picking them in their prime.

Joyce Wardwell, my friend and amazing herbalist says in her book, *The Herbal Home Remedy*, "Herbal gathering provides an intimate connection that can never come from merely buying an herb at the store". Though you can purchase fresh and dried herbs to use, the most powerful medicine comes from plants you have talked to, gathered with respect, and asked your healing requests from. Eliot Cowan, author of *Plant Spirit Medicine: The Healing Power of Plants* says, "leaves and plant parts are relatively ineffectual, it's the Spirit of the plant that does the actual healing." Before gathering plants for medicinal use, make an offering to them of tobacco, cornmeal, a bit of water, or even a short song. This ritual gives you time to state your healing requests to the Plant Devas and honors their give-away.

After picking an herb to dry, I gather the stems in one-inch bundles, secure with a rubber band, and hang them from the wooden beams in my kitchen. Hanging them upside down helps to bring the essential oils down from the stems to the leaves. Any place that is well ventilated and out of direct sunlight will do. It usually takes about three to four days for them to get crispy dry. I then break off the individual leaves, keeping them as whole as possible, and store them in airtight covered glass containers. Be sure you label the plants before you dry them, as once they are dry some look deceivingly alike. Store them in a dark pantry or kitchen cupboard.

Sometimes the best part of the plant to use is the root. Roasted dandelion root makes a beverage that reminds me of the hearty taste of coffee. The best time to gather roots is in the morning or late afternoon when the most sap is in the roots. Dig or pull them gently from the ground, remove the green tops, (which could be used in a salad), and rinse well in cold water. Chop the roots immediately into one-inch thick pieces and dry on a screen or roast in a low 200-degree oven for 2 to 3 hours or until completely dried. Again, store in an airtight, covered glass container, not plastic, as plastic fumes will eventually leach out into your product.

WAYS TO UTILIZE YOUR HERBAL MEDICINE

Like any medicine, "and herbs are medicine", it is important to use them with great care. The herbal recipes below are offered to inspire you to begin to see the gifts Nature naturally provides us, and are not given as medical advice. For health concerns, or chronic situations, it is best to consult with your personal primary health care practitioner.

HOME BREWED HERBAL TEA

Home brewed herbal tea, or "weed tea" as some of my friends call it, is one of the most nourishing gifts you can give your body. Made from healthy edible plants from your garden, I invite you to experiment with the variety of tastes and aromas you can discover.

Making an herbal infusion (its fancy name) is as easy as boiling water, stuffing a fist full of clean fresh plant material (about 2 ounces) in a tea pot, covering it with the hot water, and letting it steep for about 20 minutes. The longer you let it steep, the more medicinal energy you extract from the plant.

Once your tea has finished steeping, pour it through a fine mesh tea strainer and into your cup. There is nothing like drinking a plant's energy straight from the garden!

During the winter months, or when fresh material is not available, use the same procedure with dried herbs, reducing the amount you use to one ounce. When making tea from dried roots, simmer them in an open pan on the stovetop for 20 minutes to a full hour. Strain and enjoy!

HERBAL TINCTURES

Tinctures are another way to store the medicine of an herb for later use. Preserved in alcohol, they have a shelf life of up to five years and work well with pets, kids, when traveling, or when you are feeling too sick to go outside and gather herbs to make a tea.

To make a tincture, gather healthy fresh plant material making sure it is free from moisture. If you are using roots, wash and dry thoroughly. Chopping the herbs into smaller pieces helps to speed the process of medicine making. Fill a glass jar almost to the top with plant material, leaving about one inch for headroom. Completely cover the herb with brandy, vodka, or rum that is at least 80 proof. Insert a knife up and down into the jar several times to release any air bubbles, then add more alcohol to the top. Put on the lid and shake for at least one minute. Label and date each tincture. Double check to make sure plant material is completely covered with liquid, and add more alcohol if necessary. If exposed to the air, it will rot and spoil the tincture.

Place the jar in a dark place for 3 to 6 weeks, shaking periodically. After 3 to 6 weeks, strain the liquid through a piece of cheesecloth into a glass or stainless steel bowl or pitcher. Roll up remaining plant material in the cheese-cloth and squeeze out this precious liquid. This is where the best medicine may be found. Once completely strained, funnel into smaller dosage bottles with droppers. Label, date, and store in a cool, dark place.

Proper dosage for tinctures is one to two drops for every pound of body weight. I usually just use one dropper full to a half glass of water, depending on how strong the tincture is in taste. The standard dose is 2 to 4 times per day for six to eight weeks or longer if needed.

HERB PLANT LIST

Here is a listing of my favorite herbs. Though some of you might think of them as common weeds, I am confident they will rise to the level of food source and healer once you become better acquainted with their healing properties. The herbs I use almost daily and know intimately are as follows:

BURDOCK ROOT (*ARCTICUM LAPPA*)

Burdock, though an annoying plant to the gardener because of its long tap-root, can become a friend once you taste this root in a stir-fry or boiled like green beans. I will never starve to death in the woods if I can find a burdock root to eat. It is high in calcium, iron, and helps to eliminate toxins in the body. It can also be roasted for tea.

CALENDULA (*CALENDULA OFFICINALIS*)

Also know as pot marigold, the yellow and orange flower tops or petals are one of the best herbs for treating skin problems. It can be used safely whenever there is inflammation on the skin. Ideal for first aid treatment of minor burns and scalds, calendula oil infusion is a valuable ingredient in homemade lotions. Internally it is an effective herb for digestive inflammation or ulcers.

CATNIP (*NEPETA CATARIA*)

This is an amazing herb, whose relaxing effect on humans it quite different than what we have experienced giving it to our cats. It eases headaches and body aches, reduces fever, and is very calming during illness. I have used catnip tea to successfully lower my daughter's fever. A cloth soaked in the infusion is wonderfully soothing to place on a child's forehead. My cat loves my patch of catnip so much that in the summer I have to cover it with a wire basket. She dutifully prunes the plant as its new growth pokes through the wires and it then branches out nicely again in the fall.

CHICKWEED (*STELLARIA MEDIA*)

Chickweed is a delicate groundcover weed that you probably pull from your garden in the spring and fall. It has tiny star shaped white flowers, and is tasty as a salad green. (Again, free food!) It is a cooling herb; it softens the skin, and helps to relieve bloating. Said to aid in weight loss, it is full of vitamin C, copper, iron, and phosphorus. I have used it for eyewash for infections like pink eye and other irritations. Make an infusion in a jar of cold water in the refrigerator. After 24 hours remove the plant material from the liquid with a fine strainer and discard. Soak a washcloth or cotton ball in the remaining liquid to use as an eye compress. It is very soothing.

Mimi Ray snacking on chickweed in her garden

DANDELION (*TARRAXACUM OFFICINALE*)

Dandelion is one of the safest herbs to use, as it has no known cautionary drug interactions. All parts of the plant are edible. The flowers can be used for making wine or fritters. The leaf offers high levels of calcium, vitamin A, and minerals. The tiny knot of a bud tastes like asparagus when steamed or boiled. The roasted root has an earthy, coffee-like flavor. It is a great diuretic, aides in digestion, liver function, and stimulates bile flow. It also normalizes hormone levels. This so-called "enemy" of our lawns and chemical fertilizer companies is really a master healer!

ECHINACEA (*ECHINACEA PURPUREA*)

Herbalists consider echinacea one of the best blood purifiers, as well as an effective antibiotic. It activates the body's immune system to increase your ability to fight off diseases, and is excellent for building resistance to colds, flu, and infections. In the fall, following the start of the school season, there is often a cold bug that begins to spread itself around the community. When my daughter begins to mention a sore throat or cough, I gather fresh echinacea leaves and make her a tea. If caught early enough, you can stop a cold in its tracks this way. In the winter we use echinacea tincture that a friend has wild crafted from her garden for the same purpose. The leaves can also be frozen in clear baggies in individual doses and be made into tea.

ELDERBERRY (*SAMBUCUS CNADENSIS*)

Elderberry is full of vitamin C and has proven antiviral properties. A study in Egypt indicated that berries taken orally keep common cold and flu germs from replicating. It is important that you cook the berries of the elder before eating, as they are poisonous raw. This mild cyanide toxicity is destroyed during the cooking process. Every fall I make an elderberry cough syrup for my family to use throughout the winter. It is very tasty, and when taken early enough (when the throat first feels scratchy) it does help to ward off a cold or at least shorten it. Elderberry flowers, dried or fresh, also make an excellent tea for a sore throat, and a skin-softening facial toner. I have included a recipe for *elderberry cough syrup, among others in the next section. They are mentioned in the text with a * by them.

LAVENDER (*LAVENDULA AUGUSTIFOLIA*)

Gather lavender flowers when the petals begin to fade. The leaves may also be dried and used; though they can be bitter. Lavender sooths tension and even repels insects. Used in bath salts, cooking, and beverages, it calms nerves, relieves headaches, and sooths colic. I once hosted a lavender baby shower for a friend. We had *lavender punch, *lavender shortbread and I made a lavender herb garland for the new Mom. Needless to say it, was the most relaxing party I have ever given and all the guests were very mellow!

LAMBS QUARTER (*CHENOPODIUM*)

With the common name of pigweed, it is truly a weed among weeds! The Native Americans called it wild spinach and it has the highest calcium level of *any* of the salad greens. The seeds are also edible and can be dried and ground into a dark meal. Because of its mild flavor, I often use it in salads and enjoy just eating it right out of the garden. Find a yummy recipe for *green dressing that includes this herb in the next section.

LEMON BALM (*MELESSIA OFFICINALIS*)

The lemony scent of this herb makes it flavorful as well as medicinal. Its uplifting aroma brings comfort against despair. It eases the stress of a nervous stomach, and a lemon balm bath sooths over tired, restless children.

MONARDA (*LAMIACEAE* SPP.)

Monarda, or bee balm as it is also called, is hands down my favorite tasting herb for tea. The red and pink flowers have sweet nectar that attracts hummingbirds and bees to the garden. Use the leaves and/or flowers fresh or dried. It has been said that Monarda is a plant that helps you to learn how to love yourself.

Lavender (Lavendula augustifolia) is an aromatic and relaxing herbal addition to many recipes

MINT FAMILY (*MENTHA* SPP.)

Peppermint, spearmint, orange mint, chocolate mint – your choice, all are cooling, stimulating, and refreshing. Mints make a good summer tea as they stimulate sweating to cool the body. They are great for headaches, sinus relief, to stimulate digestion, and relieve nausea. I often add mint to other less flavorful medicinal herbs, such as thyme, to make them more palatable. This herb is *very* invasive so plant by itself, or bury in the ground in a large plastic pot with the bottom cut out to keep it contained.

MUGWORT (*ARTEMISIA VULGARIS*)

My first exposure to Mugwort was as a ***topical*** essential oil to help relieve menstrual cramps, which it does. Used externally, it also helps normalize periods and regulate blood flow. ***Mugwort is poisonous taken internally, and should never be used as a tea or tincture.*** My favorite use of this herb is to make small pillows filled with the dried plant, and tucked into my bed pillow to stimulate dreaming. It is also said to help open you to your psychic visions and abilities. Just be careful where you plant it, as its growth habit can be very invasive.

NASTURTIUM (*TROPAEOLUM MAJUS*)

These flowers add beauty and flavor to salads, and I often use them in my *garden potato salad as a colorful garnish. Its fresh leaves and flowers are most effective in the treatment of bacterial infections, especially respiratory infections like bronchitis. Drink the fresh tea three times a day for the most benefit.

NETTLES (*URTICA DIOCIA*)

This plant provides one of the highest sources of digestible iron, and is also full of calcium and vitamin A. Known also as stinging nettle, it has tiny hairs on its stem that cause a painful contact dermatitis when brushed against. I always use gloves to pick nettle but it is well worth an occasional prickly encounter. Besides, the antidote for a nettle sting is the weed plantain, which follows. Use the same application that you would for a bee sting. I have also included a *nettle soup recipe that provides wonderful nourishment as a food and a medicine.

PLANTAIN (*PLANTAGO MAJOR, P. LANCEOLATA*)

Plantain is one of those driveway weeds that almost everyone has. In fact I find it most often in driveways over any other location. There are two varieties, one with wide leaves and the other very narrow leaves. I have experimented with both and they have identical properties. Do not confuse this with the ornamental garden hosta, commonly called plantain lily. Plantain is a soothing and drawing herb, best know for helping external skin irritations. It is a favorite bee sting remedy in our home, and I speak from experience when I say it works!

Identifying this plant in your yard, or probably driveway, is helpful before the bee/wasp season begins. If you are stung, pick some leaves, masticate (chew) them in your mouth, and apply them to the stung area. A full size leaf can be used on top as a bandage, and duct tape, or nursing tape works great on top of that. I have been stung in the garden, applied this plant, and been able to continue working in a matter of minutes.

RASPBERRY (*RUBUS* SPP.)

Raspberry is known as the woman's herb. Taken throughout pregnancy it is said to ease childbirth and prevent miscarriage. High in calcium, it also helps ease menstrual cramping. I like to gather raspberry on the Spring and Fall Equinox. Dried, it is one of my favorite wintertime teas.

ROSE (*ROSA RUGOSA.*)

Old-fashioned highly scented roses, or wild roses, are better suited for medicine than the fancy hybrid plants. Roses, whether in fresh or dried form, add a delicate flavor and energy to your preparations. Rose petals are at their peak when the center of the flower is still yellow, before it turns brown. Rose hips picked after the first hard frost can be used as a tea, and are extremely high in vitamin C. They also dry well.

THYME (*THYMUS VULGARIS*)

Thyme, though well know as a culinary herb, is less know for it's outstanding anti-viral and anti-microbial properties. It is used to treat viral infections and to help boost the immune system. A thyme infusion bath along with a cup of hot thyme tea is one of your best herbal defenses against the common cold. Thyme is also useful to cleanse external cuts and wounds.

Thyme, a most beautiful and useful herb. I love to affirm "I have plenty of thyme in my garden"

VIOLET (*VIOLA. ODORATA, V. TRICOLOR HORTENSIS*)

Common purple sweet violets (*V. odorata*) with small heart-shaped leaves are the types I grow in my garden. These beauties are said to be one of the best-known herbal allies for breast cancer. Fill a quart jar with dried or fresh chopped leaves and cover with boiling water. Strain and drink two cups of tea each day.

One ounce of violet leaves contains five times more vitamin C than one ounce of fresh orange juice and three times more vitamin A. The flowers of either species, sweet violets or pansys (*V. tricolor hortensis*), make colorful and healthy additions to tossed salads.

WOOD SORREL (*OXALIS ACETOSELLA*)

Wood Sorrel has characteristic tiny yellow flowers and a clover-shaped leaf. This is another weed I was constantly pulling from the garden before I tasted it. The lemon flavored flowers and leaves add just the right tang to a garden salad. These tiny banana shaped seedpods make a tasty lemon-flavored snack that is popular with children. This member of the shamrock family quenches thirst and reduces fever. It is a blood cleanser, and also strengthens a weak stomach and helps to produce an appetite.

HERBAL GARDEN RECIPES

Below are a few of my favorite recipes using the herbs I grow in the garden. I use fresh herbs whenever possible, but feel free to substitute dried when necessary.

❧ CHICKWEED WATER ❧

Fill a large clear glass jar or beverage dispenser full of fresh water. Add three to four cups of fresh chickweed. Let sit overnight in the refrigerator. Serve cold. You can also substitute any fresh herb of your choice; mint, monarda, oregano, and thyme all lend their distinctive tastes. A mixture is fun too. Just experiment! You can continually refill the jar containing the herbs with fresh water and store in the refrigerator for up to one week. (This recipe works best with fresh plant material.)

❧ LAVENDER PUNCH ❧

Combine together equal parts white grape juice and a strong lavender tea infusion and chill. Place in punch bowl with ice cubes made from short sprigs of lavender flowers added to the water in each cube tray.

❧ LAVENDER SHORTBREAD ❧

8 ounces unsalted butter
4 teaspoons fresh lavender buds or 2 teaspoons dried
½ cup sugar
2 cups flour

Soften butter by removing from refrigerator fifteen minutes before starting. Place the lavender buds and the sugar together in a blender or small food processor and grind until fine. Transfer the lavender sugar to a mixing bowl with the softened butter. Beat at low speed with an electric mixer until mixture is smooth: do not beat until fluffy. Add all the flour at once and continue to mix on low speed just until it forms a cohesive dough. Turn the dough out onto a lightly floured surface, press it firmly into a smooth rectangular block with no cracks and dust it lightly with more flour. Using a rolling pin, roll in into a 9 by 12-inch rectangle, ¼ inch thick, rotating the dough a quarter turn each time you roll it to make sure it is not sticking to the work surface. Using a straight edge or pastry wheel, cut the dough into 2 by 1 ½ inch bars, or cut out other shapes with cookie cutters. Using a spatula, transfer the cookies onto a baking sheet lined with parchment paper, leaving ½ inch space between them. Refrigerate the cookies 30 minutes to allow dough to rest.

Preheat the oven to 300 degrees. Bake the cookies until they are light sandy color, not browned, 22 to 25 minutes. Let the cookies cool completely before removing from pan.

Yields 24 cookies.

❧ MINNIE'S GARDEN POTATO SALAD ❧

3 pounds potatoes, pealed, boiled, and cubed

5–6 hard boiled eggs, peeled and chopped

¾ cup mayonnaise

2 tablespoons yellow table mustard

1 cup blanched asparagus (boil for one minute then rinse in cold water)

½ cup chopped carrots

½ cup chopped celery

½ chopped green pepper

1 small onion chopped

1 clove garlic chopped

1 handful fresh parsley chopped

2 sprigs fresh dill chopped

4 sprigs of fresh tarragon chopped

5 stems of fresh chives chopped

Salt and ground pepper to taste

Pansies, violets, calendulas and/or nasturtiums for garnish

Peel potatoes and boil until cooked. Cut up into ½ inch cubes. Add chopped hardboiled egg, carrots, asparagus, green pepper and celery. Add mayonnaise and mustard; mix until well coated. Blend in chopped herbs, season to taste. Place in decorative bowl and garnish with fresh flowers.

❧ HERBAL GREEN DRESSING ❧

1 cup safflower oil (or light flavored oil)
2 tablespoons apple cider vinegar (or fresh lemon juice)
1 teaspoon honey (or 2 tablespoons apple juice)
5 or 6 spinach leaves
20 lambs quarter leaves
2 tablespoons chopped parsley
½ teaspoon salt
1 to 4 cloves garlic
1 cup buttermilk
1 teaspoon fresh basil
1 teaspoon fresh marjoram
Or ½ cup herb mix of your choice

Place everything except the buttermilk in blender, puree for 1 minute. Add the buttermilk, blend until mixed. Chill 30 minutes. Enjoy the beautiful spring green color and taste.

❧ ELDERBERRY COUGH SYRUP ❧

9 cups elder berries
½ cup water
½ cup local honey
¼ cup brandy

Identify elder shrubs in your area by the white blossoms in the early summer; they like low-lying wet areas. Watch closely for the purple berries to appear in late summer because you will have competition from the birds. Gather berry bracts and make the syrup that same day, or freeze berries for later use.

In a large pot on the stove place washed berries still on the bracts and ½ cup of water. Simmer on low until berries begin to fall off, remove stems that are free of berries. After most of the berries have fallen off, drain the liquid into another pot covered with cheesecloth. After berry bracts have cooled to the touch, wrap in the cheesecloth and squeeze out any remaining juice. Combine all of the strained juice into one large pot. Add honey and stir until it has dissolved. Turn off stove. Add brandy as the final ingredient. Stir and then funnel into clean storage jars. I have found dark glass recycled maple syrup containers work well. Store in the refrigerator for up to 6 months.

Dosage: 1 tablespoon 4–5 times daily as needed for cold and flu.

❧ CREAMY NETTLE SOUP ❧

10 cups stinging nettle leaves
2 leaks (chopped white and some green parts)
1 yellow onion chopped
1 russet potato peeled and chopped
2 stalks of celery chopped
4 tablespoons of butter or olive oil
2 ½ cups of vegetable stock or water
salt and pepper to taste

Melt butter or heat oil in a soup pan. Add chopped vegetables and nettle leaves. On medium heat, cover and let the vegetables cook down for about five minutes. Add the water or stock and simmer for about 20 minutes. Puree in blender or food processor. Serve with sour cream. This soup travels and serves well in a crockpot.

⤸ VIOLET MOON WATER ⤸

Make this water on a night of the full moon to call in violet's magical powers of protection, love, peace and healing. Place an amethyst stone in a crystal glass. Fill the glass with violet blossoms and pure water. Leave out in the moonlight overnight. In the morning remove the amethyst and flowers and drink the water; half at that time, and half before retiring in the evening.

⤸ INFUSED HERBAL OIL ⤸

Herbal oils are wonderful to cook with; use them for stir-frying or to make homemade salad dressings. They are also the perfect medicinally infused ingredient to incorporate into homemade lotions and balms. These make great gifts.

The easiest and most traditional way of making infused oil is to fill a clean and sterile jar with fresh herbs and cover the herbs with your choice of oil. I use light olive oil for cooking and salad dressings, and jojoba oil or almond oil for skin care products. What is most important is covering the plant material completely with the oil to keep oxygen from rotting it and encouraging bacteria to grow.

Place the oil somewhere where you will notice it often, and give it a gentle shake once a day for three to six weeks. After the herb's energy and scent have infused in the oil, run it through a sieve to remove the solid plant material, and transfer to a decorative container if desired. Infused oils have a shelf life of about three months and make great gifts. Refrigeration will double their shelf life.

❧ HERBAL FACE LOTION ❧

It is a good idea when making your own lotions and salves to have kitchen equipment set aside just for this use. I have an older blender with a lid you can pour through, saucepan, and wooden spoon reserved just for this purpose. All of the ingredients below can be found at your local health food store.

STEP ONE

¾ cup apricot, almond, or grape seed oil infused with herb of your choice

⅓ cup coconut oil

1 teaspoon lanolin

½ ounce grated beeswax

STEP TWO

⅔ cup distilled water (or rose or orange water)

⅓ cup aloe vera gel

3–5 drops of essential oil of choice

3 drops vitamin A or E to prevent bacterial growth

Stir Step One ingredients over low heat to melting point. Let cool to room temperature.

Place Step Two ingredients in a blender. Turn on high speed. Pour cooled oil mixture from Step One into center of vortex in blender at a slow drizzle. When blender coughs and chokes and mixture looks like butter cream frosting, you are done. Do not over mix (adapted from Rosemary Gladstars' recipe in *Herbal Healing for Women*).

CHAPTER 7

GARDEN
AS HEALER

੭

A connection with Nature allows us to move through the earthly emotions of love, fear, and grief with a sense of support and sustenance. Through experiencing the life and death cycles of the plants, we are once again reminded of our own immortality. The gift Nature gives us is the total acceptance of these cycles as a part of our time here. It is neither good nor bad, it just *is*.

MOM'S STROKE

Gardens can provide us unexpected ways to extend our love and healing. On the warm July morning my mother had a stroke I was at a loss about what to do. Dad had died only a year earlier, and the fear of facing death again weighed heavy on my mind. I had only recently found a balance for the feelings of grief I was working through from losing Dad, how could I possibly be asked to start all over again with Mom?

Moving beyond this initial fear, the next question was what could I do for Mom, right now, in the present moment? The answer came loudly and clearly, "Go, just be *with* her." I sensed she would be frightened and unhappy. She had

Long lasting hydrangea blooms bring the healing color of purple to the garden

a great dislike for hospitals, doctors, and all their tests. And because they were unsure of what really had happened to her, there were bound to be plenty of tests in her future. So I decided to put my life on hold and just go.

Before leaving to make the two-hour drive, the one item I am forever grateful for taking the time to bring was a huge bouquet of perennials picked from my Cottage Garden. I walked through the beds with my pruning shears asking the Garden Devas which flowers wanted to be with Mom. The ones that said, "Yes," responded by shining brighter than their neighbors or catching my eye in some other way. When I finished, I had gathered a beautiful arrangement of lilies, delphinium, daisies, coreopsis, and more. All her favorites, and all so exquisite and positively glowing in the clear glass vase I had selected.

Driving straight to the hospital entrance the scent of flowers still filling the car, I grabbed the vase and went searching for her room. With my face almost hidden by this amazing bouquet of exploding color, I walked through her door; and through the stems, I could see her genuinely surprised face. As she slurred the word "flowers!" the whole room brightened. Her beaming eyes smiled with joy and in that moment I knew why I had come; to share these healing gifts of Nature with her.

After only a few minutes, to my relief, it was clear that other than vocal expression she had all the rest of her other faculties intact. With "Yes" and "No" being the only words spoken clearly, we spent a lot of time learning to communicate in new ways, with a lot of body language thrown in. I loved just being there with her; watching television together, reading while she slept. There is such love and peace in just being present with someone.

During her three days in the hospital, and in between tests, she often wanted to go walking in the halls. Being a volunteer at this particular facility, Mom knew right where to find the most beautiful view of the hospital garden. The only problem was that she was on a heart monitor, and every time we went to this window we were out of reading range from the nurses station. Their monitors would go off and we would get scolded for going too far. But do you think this stopped us from visiting that garden again?

Mother's room just happened to be the same one Dad had had a heart attack in, a year earlier. I'm not sure Mom realized this, but I did and would often look over at the extra bed and feel his presence with us. It remained empty until the very last night she was to stay there; right after she was told she could go home in the morning!

We learned that the woman who took 'Dad's bed' had no family, and had been in and out of this hospital a lot lately. It was Mom's idea to leave the sweet smelling flowers for her quiet neighbor to enjoy. I took the vase across the room to the woman's bedside table, saying we were leaving them for her, and her eyes filled with light. She was overjoyed, and the flowers had a second chance to do their magic!

Driving Mom home to her garden that summer morning was such a treat. I will never forget how happy she looked, hanging her head out of the rolled-down car window, filling her face with fresh air and the sun. Of course the first place she wanted to go, even before entering the house, was her garden. She had been gone for three days, a lot had happened in her absence! As I write this I'm happy to say that Mom is still gardening, and her outlook on life is a positive and grateful one, happy to just have one more day in the garden with her flowers. And I am grateful too, for the gifts from the garden that I was able to share with her during this trying time.

NATURES RESILIENCY

I am forever awed by the resiliency of Nature and its ability to bounce back – usually with twice as much gusto – when confronted with change. Prune any plant back a few inches and just watch what happens. Where once there was a single branch, is now a multiple of two or three, given a little time. Thoreau spoke, in *Walden's Pond,* about how the forest was always trying to swallow up his garden, like a huge monster with a voracious appetite for any open cleared land.

My first lesson working with Nature on a grand scale happened shortly after moving from the city to the countryside. We had purchased a small ranch home on five acres of hardwoods and pines. The street we lived on was named Bewell, which I always called "Be well", and was designated as a Natural Beauty Road. Huge oak trees grew at the roads edges, their branches reaching out to one another forming a London Bridge-type canopy overhead. Pink and white dogwood trees bloomed profusely in the spring, and blue lupine, chicory, and assorted wildflowers fringed the roadside.

After only two months of living along this beautiful dirt and gravel road, I was told plans were already underway to pave it! My heart ached with sadness, not only because they were paving it, but also because this required them to widen the road by at least five feet on each side. This meant the removal of over one hundred large hardwood trees on a stretch of road less than one mile long; so much for Natural Beauty Road status! I talked with the Township Board, went to Road Commission meetings, and wrote letters to the editor in the local paper. It seemed I was the only voice the trees had, and I was losing a battle started way too late.

As the trees were marked with the fateful x's of orange spray paint, I became resigned to watching man destroy Nature in the name of "progress" for the millionth time. My only solace was that three large hundred-year-old oaks marking the entrance to my driveway were spared from the chainsaws. To appease me, the township rerouted the road plans an additional five feet into the open field opposite my home, and these three impressive trees were to remain untouched. Perhaps the supervisor conceded this to me for fear I would be the type who would chain myself to the trees causing all kinds of trouble.

The day they decided to spare my trees reminds me of a famous starfish story. It goes like this: A boy is walking on the beach and discovers a huge numbers of starfish have washed up on the shore because of a recent storm. The boy starts picking them up and throwing them back into the water one by one. Someone tells him it is useless, he will never make a difference, there are just too many to save. The boy replies, after tossing another one in," I just made a difference for that one"

Even now, as I drive by those *Three Awesome Magnificent Oak Trees* that are forever changing, I know that I made a difference for them. I may have lost

The Three Magnificent Oak
Trees the road was moved
over to accommodate

the battle to save the road from being paved, but I did win the lives of those trees. It was worth speaking my truth.

There was also a lot I did before the "cut" day, including some things you could also do in similar situations. First, once I knew I had "lost" and there was no turning back the chainsaws, I walked up and down the street talking with all the trees, shrubs, and flowers that I knew were destined to be destroyed. I asked *all* the Nature Spirits or Devas in that vicinity to *move back* at least five feet from the edge of the road. Even now, if I see areas being prepared for development, I always do the same thing. My motto for any plant removal and/or disruption is to talk to the Nature Spirits to give them as much prior notice as possible.

My son and I also collected acorns and seeds from the fated trees and planted them in the fields and "safe" areas around our home. This felt proactive and ensured that at least some of those ancient trees would live on, even though my heart was still grieving for what was to come.

On that day, when over one hundred trees were cut, I felt deep anguish in my Soul. I stood and watched, faithfully guarding my three oaks in case someone hadn't gotten the message they were not to be touched. I still have vivid memories of watching so many awesome trees surrendering so easily to man's machines.

When the workmen took their hour-long lunch break, and left the street impassible with fallen logs, I took my 5-year-old son out to see the destruction. I wanted him to witness with his own eyes and heart what man can do so quickly to the environment. I remember placing my hand on a freshly cut oak stump, and feeling the pulsing energy pumping up from it. Our worst experience that summer day was hearing a mother bird frantically looking for her nest in a fallen tree. We tried to help her find it, but to no avail. I tell this sad story to emphasize the emotion we as humans bring to such a situation. Nature was just doing what she has always done, giving to us all that we ask for without judgment.

Thirteen years later, blacktopped Bewell Road has been designated as a Natural Beauty Road again. The oak trees at its edges are beginning to reach across to one another to form an overhead canopy. You can still see beautiful dogwood blooming along the roadside in the spring, as Nature has taken over again to fill in all the gaps. There are no residues of anger or grudges, just Nature doing what it does best with a little room, water and sunshine: GROW!

Like a tree that grows in the crack of a city sidewalk, it is a force that is unstoppable. When naysayers talk about the end of the world, I still see Nature as adaptable and prevailing. Provoked by our own doing, the earth may someday shake us off her back like the fleas we have become. Over time the sidewalks and buildings and junk we left behind will be completely hidden under the lush green growth of life. Nature will swallow us up, just like the Mayan ruins were thousands of years ago, and the cycle will continue. Again, it is not "Save the Planet" that I am most concerned about; it is "Save the Humans" from ourselves!

Know there is a resiliency to Nature, and given time and a little help from us, forests can be reclaimed, trees can be planted, and new gardens can grow in places we have ravaged. When we heal the wounds of the earth, we in turn are healing ourselves.

SEPTEMBER 11, 2001

It is September 11, 2001. I am finally home from an early morning dentist appointment and running errands. I guess everyone remembers where he or she were when they heard the horrific news. . . I was sitting in the dentist chair having my teeth cleaned. It was on the radio; the report of the Pentagon being hit while the hygienist looked wide eyed into mine and said, "Oh my God!"

Listening to the surreal radio reports of the events in the car, I finally arrive home, and eagerly, and at the same time reluctantly, turn on the television. Now I have a real life visual of those two skyscrapers tumbling to their death, and imagine those inside. I sit in a trance watching the screen for hours. Numb, I switch off the television, and head out the front door to my garden.

It is a beautiful late summer afternoon. The frogs are out in numbers sunning themselves at the pond, oblivious to the day's events. The flowers still greet me with shining faces, and I feel safe and centered at least here in my own private oasis, sheltered for a moment from the happenings of the world. My heart hurts, I am unsure of what tomorrow may bring, but in this moment, time stands still as the warmth of the sun wraps me in a kaleidoscope of colorful blooms and deep summer scents. My garden continues, life goes on, and there is still order in my corner of the world. If I were to die today, this is the last view of earth I would most long to see. Garden as healer, I am protected by its energy.

Fragrant white
Casa blanca lilies

HARMONIC CONCORDANCE 2003

It is November 8, 2003; an unusual astrological alignment of five planets, along with the sun and the moon, will form the shape of the Star of David tonight. Along with this amazing feat, a total lunar eclipse will occur. In Michigan, it is scheduled to begin about 5:30 PM and move through the last hours of the evening.

I bundle up in winter coat, hat, and gloves to face the frosty twenty-eight degrees outside. My family has joined me to experience this rare opportunity; to witness a moment in history they will remember all their lives. The sky is clear and bright, filled with the luminous glow of the moon beginning to shift from full to three-quarters before our very eyes. As we watch in awe at this beauty, the heavens gift us with shooting stars and planets that are clearly visible. My children witness the great mystery of the universe, and I am relishing the joy I see on their faces. Shivering, we remain glued to our claimed viewing spots on the blanket in the driveway, occasionally taking a closer look with the shared binoculars. I have always thought the moon looks like Victorian lace when seen this close, and tonight is no exception.

As the Earth's shadow covers over half of the moon's surface, we each say our prayers out loud for the coming year. This is our time to project into the future the dreams we have on our minds today. One of my prayers is to see the completion of the book you are reading. We seal our prayers with a chant, and continue to watch a red glow cover the shadowed side of the moon. Native peoples used to believe that during a total eclipse the jaguar was swallowing the moon, this red tint must have reminded them of blood. When the entire moon is completely in shadow and glowing red we say our final prayers of gratitude and retreat to the warmth indoors.

Late into the night I am finally heading to bed. I have just opened a disturbing email, telling me that my good friend Phyllis has recently been admitted into hospice care and is not expected to live much longer. I am feeling guilt and sadness over not spending more time with her. If only I had given her more attention, done more feng shui, more ceremony with her maybe she would not be on this threshold.

Walking past the front door, I see the garden absolutely glowing in moonlight. It draws me outside for the second time that night. Bundling up in my housecoat and son's large warm boots, I go and sit on the front steps. The moon is even more spectacular than earlier, glowing as if from within. I feel it pulling me closer to it with every breath I take. The gardens, though stiff and brown, are bathed in this luminescent spotlight. I gaze in wonder, and ask why my friend has to be leaving all this beauty. The reply, coming from grandmother moon and the Nature Devas, is that this is the perfect time for her to go. Of course!

Earlier that evening I had told the kids it was a great time to be born; yet, I had not thought about the opposite – of making transitions. During this harmonic concordance, portals for astral travel are opened wide. In fact, I believe Phyllis intentionally waited until this time, which is why her dance with cancer lasted so long. At that moment, I realized it was completely out of my hands; in fact it never was in them! The great plan had already been set in motion, one her Soul orchestrated many years ago.

Gazing upward, I could feel this portal opening, as the thickness of the moon pulled me near. I could see her spirit riding on this wave, making her transition with ease and grace. I was no longer worried about my friend, but in awe of her strong Spirit and her decision to depart at this most auspicious time. I went to bed that night with a deep peace filling my being, knowing that all was in perfect order.

We had six close family members and friends make their transition during the month following the harmonic concordance. The wisdom I received from the garden on that beautiful moon-filled night allowed me to accept their choices with a peace-filled heart.

The garden is my constant, my solace – even in the winter when all seems to be sleeping. I can still feel its energy, and derive strength from this abundant life force flowing just beneath the surface. Nature grieves with me and heals me all at the same time. Garden as healer helps me see that with death also comes new life.

CHAPTER 8

GARDENS OF INSPIRATION

⌁

Gardens can be created anywhere, for almost any purpose. In fact, the more intention you place into a garden for its purpose, the more you will receive from it. Naming offers even more intention and sacredness to a space. Native Americans believe giving something a name births it into being, honoring its unique qualities.

Here are some of the unique gardens I have "birthed into being".

Simple petunias have a beauty all their own

BALCONY GARDENS AND TERRACES

I have always had a garden, even during the first years of my marriage when I lived in a city apartment and had no land to call my own. At that time I worked at a floral and garden center, and there were always plants that needed homes. Often digging in the dumpster, I rescued many a forlorn plant, cut back the old growth, and revived it to its full glory.

Our tiny second-story balcony was located on the southeast side of the building, with just room enough for two chairs. Yet flowers and plants of all colors and kinds spilled over the railings and climbed up to the sky. This was such a stark contrast to the plain brown walls and cement patios of our surrounding neighbors; a few graced with the occasional geranium or lonely tomato in a pot. Outdoors on my balcony were hanging baskets of yellow black-eyed susan vines, purple ivy geraniums, and fuchsia plants. Hot pink sweet peas climbed a trellis propped in a container filled with herbs and vegetables. Gloxinias, daisies, marigolds, and ferns filled every available bit of space. It glowed to greet me from the parking lot after a long day of working, making me smile. I was so happy to be home.

One day I arrived home from work to see hundreds of bees swarming the patio door to the balcony. This balcony had so much color and vitality that it had attracted an entire hive of honeybees and their queen. I had created a garden filled with their every need there in the city! They took up residence in a wooden wine crate I used as a plant stand leaning against the wall. Not wanting to destroy them, but knowing it would be impossible to live with them, I called the Entomology department of nearby Michigan State University. Put in touch with a Professor Eberly, a honeybee expert, I explained my situation and he agreed to come the following Sunday night to pick up the bees. Apparently their systems slow down in cooler weather and he wanted to take advantage of the falling evening temperatures in order to remove them safely.

He arrived in an old blue Chevy station wagon, with his entire family all dressed in their Sunday best. They were just returning from a friend's graduation party and thought they'd pick up the bees on their way home! Eberly put a bee hat on, confidently walked out to the balcony, picked up the crate, and proceeded to casually walk through our apartment, buzzing hive, crate, and all! Because the queen honeybee was inside the crate, the rest of the bees dutifully followed her. He then placed the boisterous crate in the back of the station wagon, thanked us for the hive, and off they drove!

CONTAINER GARDENS

Container gardens, like the ones I attracted the bees with, also have several positive attributes. They have their own soil, which can easily be amended when it needs a boost of organic material or new compost. They can easily be moved around to follow the sun, or to add color to a dull spot in the garden. And, they can be placed where soil cannot – like on a cement patio, wooden deck, or other hardscape surface. I have even seen pots skillfully placed within the garden, adding color and height to areas quickly and easily. A friend incorporates pots of shade-loving impatiens within her beds of groundcover under the trees. The flowers planted in containers do not have to compete for space or light with the dense carpet of vinca below, and add a bright touch of color to an otherwise all green landscape.

Hanging plants also offer this variety and a chance to add color to the landscape. My favorite place for a hanging plant is from a tree limb. There is something natural and yet surprising about seeing a bright spot of color so high on the garden horizon. It helps the Chi to flow upward as well. And in special instances, they create gathering screens of plant life that help to contain the Chi flow in that specific area.

If there are no sturdy tree limbs available, try a single or double shepherds hook. These are tall metal rods with curved hanging hooks. They can be placed anywhere and create an immediate backdrop of greenery and color for any spot that needs some height. I have one placed behind a sitting bench in the abundance garden with a beautiful hot pink and purple fuchsia hanging from it. The plants below the fuchsia are in full shade, yet the height of the hook puts this hanging plant in a much sunnier location. It not only helps contain escaping Chi flow from the steep bank, but also provides the "mountain" feeling of support from behind as you relax on the bench.

I have been experimenting with unique combinations of container gardens on my deck for the past several years. One year I planted all herb pots with just a few annuals for color. The basil and variegated thyme looked beautiful in contrast to the hot pink fuchsia, bright yellow marigolds, and blue lobelia. Another year I planted according to the Bagua map placement. In the Partnership corner of the deck I placed a pot filled with pink blooming plants with round or heart shaped leaves. In the Fame area were red flowers and spiky leaf shapes. In the Wealth corner purple and lavender colors of course, and plants with many flowers.

Gardener Rebecca Cole has written two fantastic books on this subject, *Potted Gardens: A Fresh Approach to Container Gardening* and *Paradise Found: Gardening in Unlikely Places.* Her philosophy is to keep what she calls "A small palette of colors," when working with a small space, like a deck or rooftop garden. This means using one or two different colors plus the greenery. That's all!

It is in the variety of textures and flower shapes within that color palette that the garden comes alive. Being an all over the color wheel type of gardener, this idea was difficult for me at first. I tried it on the deck one year, limiting myself to a peaceful design of only yellow and purple and blue tones. Oh, how I desperately wanted to add some red or some peach. I even planted up a pot of peachy orange begonias to give it what I thought was that necessary splash of color. Yet Cole was right; it didn't work! My eye went only to that single orange flower, it stuck out like a sore thumb. When I removed it, the soft flow of yellows, lavenders, and blues, in a background of cooling shades of green, felt soft and restful again.

I understand the concept now, after experimenting for myself. Sometimes that is the best way to learn, by trying it and *feeling* the difference. I discovered that using so many colors in such a small space creates scattered and jumpy Chi. The Chi slows down to a steady and restful pace when in comparison a shorter color palette is utilized. There is always a feng shui explanation for what you are feeling in the environment, if you only look for it!

Using a "short color palette" for the containers on the deck brings continuity to a small space

Thinking outside the box of conventional container planting can be fun and creative. Putting together combinations you may have never dreamed of can bring about interesting and unexpected results. A six-foot tall river birch from the nursery, with pansies or ivy from the greenhouse planted at its base, gives my deck some much needed height and helps to create a green wall between the eating area and the lounging side. The ivy helps to anchor the tree into the container and softens the harsh edge of the pot, without causing too much busyness. A yellow blooming cinquefoil surrounded by lavender violas is a treat to watch blooming all summer. Having shrubs on the deck may be a new playful concept for you to use in creating outdoor spaces.

Blending together ordinary houseplants with nursery items, perennials, shrubs, and annuals opens up several new combinations of plant material. Mix them up; play with their textures and shapes. There is no wrong combination of these categories. Treat the houseplants like annuals, shrubs like container plants. How beautiful to see the delicate blooms of spirea or lilac up close and personal on a terrace garden in the spring.

When I saw what Cole was planting on rooftops in New York City, and the plants were surviving the high winds and harsh winters there, I thought surely they would work in Michigan, too. Her trick is to wrap plastic or winter hardy pots in bubble wrap and then burlap for tasteful protection from freezing and thawing temperatures.

Window boxes and their plant combinations can be filled with these new combinations as well. One requirement I always have in my boxes is to have something drape over the edge and flow downward. A box of all upright plants looks unnatural and contrived. Always fill it with more plants than you think necessary for a lived-in look from day one.

Window boxes give you double enjoyment, as they are visible from the exterior and interior of the home. Sometimes they are even easier to water from inside the house. Often clients have narrow side yards that are not conducive to placing a garden there. I often recommend a window box instead to help activate that area of the bagua.

ABUNDANCE MIRROR GARDEN

One spring, a client I'll call Diane, hired me for a feng shui and garden consultation. She and her husband had moved from California, and in her words, "For the last seven years it just feels like we've been losing money. Right now my husband is making ¼ of what he used to make in California. I've had some new business ideas to help, but nothing has come to fruition. It is so frustrating. So, with great reluctance, my husband said okay to bringing in your expertise! I feel like something needs to be done."

Several "red flags" went up the minute I began meditating with her house and site plan. For one, she lived at the end of a T-zone with strong Chi from the street flying straight into her front door. She also had small missing pieces in Career and Helpful people. The biggest challenge I felt was a draining away of energy off the back Wealth area of the home and property. There was nothing visibly wrong with this space; the Wealth area was intact and part of a large living room. I thought perhaps the home was on a high hill and the Chi might be flowing strongly away from this area of her home.

When I arrived and took a walk around the house, I immediately saw what I had been feeling. The Wealth section of Diane's property, and the yard that hugged the Wealth corner of her home, was a low area covered with large-size gravel stones. She proceeded to tell me that there was a storm drain under the gravel that caught the water flow from both back and front yards. Because she could not plant a garden here, my creative feng-shui mind had to kick into high gear. Some type of deflection was needed; as all that water, a symbol of wealth and Chi flow, was literally draining away into the sewers. I came up with the idea of planting a mirror garden here, to send the positive Chi flow right back into the house.

Diane's mirror garden consisted of several mirror balls on pedestals of different heights. These garden globes were visually anchored next to a large planter filled with purple blooming flowers and trailing plants. In order to keep this arrangement out year-round, Diane purchased unbreakable stainless steel balls that could be left out in the winter. In the fall she fills the planter with fresh cut evergreen and red berries so that it has color year round.

Six months after our initial consultation, Diane called me to say thank you and informed me that her husband now had the job of his dreams, working from home, and that his salary had increased dramatically. She was also happy to tell me she had started on a creative book project that she now finally had found the time and energy for. Her husband is still not quite sure what or how the feng shui adjustments made the difference in their lives; he is just happy they did.

CHILDREN'S GARDENS

As I begin writing on the subject of children's gardens, I want to make it clear I do not mean gardens designed by adults, for children to play in. I am referring to a children's garden that is wholly created with the ideas and spirit of a child. It is amazing what happens to a child when given their very own piece of land to cultivate. They look at it with such different eyes than a "seasoned adult," and in that comes the fun! The greatest gift I give my daughter or son when sharing my love of gardening with them is to stay out of their way. Letting them discover how things grow on their own has been one of the most difficult, and also most rewarding, tasks I have attempted. And I still say attempt, because I often have to bite my tongue when wanting to offer advice or suggestions.

When my son Stephan was about five years old, he asked for his own garden. When asked what he wanted to grow, he replied, "Those flowers that poof." He was referring to my friend the dandelion, a plant I was more often digging up for its roots rather than planting! Don't get me wrong, I love dandelions and their amazing medicinal properties, I had just never thought of intentionally "planting" them anywhere.

Yet because he had his heart set on them, I proceeded to move every one I found in other areas of the garden to his small plot of land. He often helped me with the transplanting and watering. Needless to say with all that "extra" attention they thrived, and soon we had a small patch of bright yellow blossoms that he impatiently waited to turn into his favorite toys of Nature. Joyfully he ran around the yard and blew those dandelion seeds into the wind.

His garden fulfilled his desire, and provided him with lots of free entertainment that summer.

In the spring, when my daughter Jessica was eight, she began to plan her own flower garden. She enjoys growing things from seed and her favorites are sunflowers, zinnias, and morning glories. The plant she excels at, though, is larkspur. In the Cottage Garden mine grows to about two to three feet tall, while hers reach nearly five feet with stems as big around as her thumb! They re-seed themselves every year, and all she does is thin them out. Sometimes, if I am lucky, she shares her extras; but when I transplant them to my garden, they are still never as robust as hers. Perhaps the Nature Spirits in the garden love the attention of children, and, in turn, put on an extra show for them.

Stephan, who is studying now to be a Landscape Architect, is the caretaker for an interesting garden of his own design. He is interested in native plantings and xeriscaping, so he has a test plot near the larkspurs. Xeriscaping is the practice of growing a rich array of drought-tolerant native species that need little maintenance and that mimic the natural plants found in a bioregion. He basically cultivates, if you could call it that, what is already present or that chooses to grow there. He grows wild cinquefoil, plantain, motherwort, aster, and sumac all in this small 3 by 5 foot space. He does have wild morning glories growing up a tree stump, and occasionally plants a native perennial like purple coneflowers (*Echinacea*) or a mallow species for some added color. It is hard, as Mom the gardener, to not want to weed his weeds; yet I resist. Besides, he would know instantly if even one plant were out of place. His *is* the easiest garden to care for, and the most drought resistant I have noticed.

So, let the kids have their own space to learn Nature's lessons. Yes, in the past I have spent money on doomed plants that they "had to have" – that disliked growing in the shade or in bright sunlight; yet that is how they learn to really understand a plants needs. And, my kids have taught me so much about going against "the rules". One year Stephan planted orange and red begonias with hot pink impatiens, a color scheme I would have never tried! It was beautiful! So have fun with your kids, and let them be in charge. You just might be inspired by their creative minds.

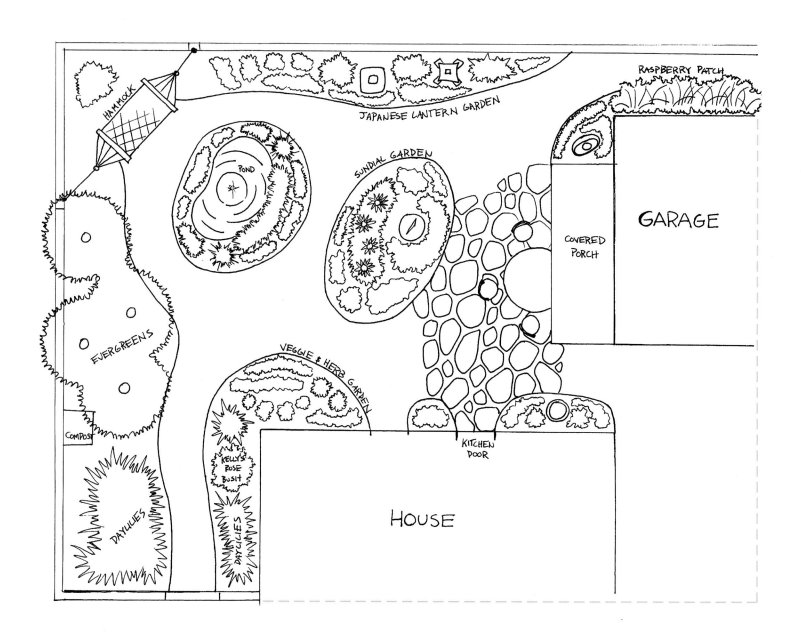

RASPBERRY PATCH

GARAGE

COVERED PORCH

JAPANESE LANTERN GARDEN

SUNDIAL GARDEN

POND

HAMMOCK

EVERGREENS

COMPOST

VEGGIE & HERB GARDEN

KELLY'S ROSE BUSH

DAYLILIES

DAYLILIES

KITCHEN DOOR

HOUSE

OUTDOOR ROOMS

One summer I worked with a client who lived in an older suburban neighborhood. She was bored and tired of the typical patch of grass in her backyard, and her husband was tired of mowing it. I suggested she fill it all in with garden instead. After having a brand new fence installed she had me visit for the initial consultation.

We looked at the bagua layout over just the backyard for this garden. The Mouth of Chi was determined by the most frequent entrance she used to get there, her kitchen door. That meant standing in this doorway and looking out, the middle of her back fence area was in Fame, the right hand corner was the Partnership area, and the far left back corner became the Wealth area. (See diagram on page 144.)

Deciding that it would be fun to create a series of outdoor rooms, we then determined what elements and energies would be most supportive for each of these spaces. For instance, the "Japanese Garden Room", located in the Fame area along the fence, would have a collection of stone lanterns to symbolize the fire element there.

A meandering path was drawn in first, to stimulate the Chi flow lines from room to room. This movement helped to create the different outdoor room placements.

Stepping out from the kitchen, one's eye is drawn immediately back to the Japanese Garden Room situated along the fence. The stone lantern lights easily turned on from a switch located inside the house. There is an oriental "look" to the plantings here and a simplistic style. Some larger boulders were buried four to five inches into the ground with only their tops showing to symbolically represent mountains. Small ornamental trees, vibrant orange-red daylilies, and vines growing on the fence contribute to the feeling of Fire Chi rising upward.

Stepping-stones take you to the right and behind the garage to the secret Raspberry Patch. On the way you also find a hidden Buddha Garden in the Partnership area. Sweet woodruff is an excellent ground cover here in the shade and provides a nice backdrop for the pink impatiens. Coming back to the patio area in Children and Creativity, you may want to sit down for dinner at the black wrought iron table representing the element for this gua, Metal. Brightly colored pillows and cushions are on the chairs. The Sundial Garden, located in the Health area, is filled with sunny perennials and annuals, and readily captures the attention of dinner guests. In this garden, taller plants like helenium and yellow sunflower are planted as a backdrop. They intentionally block your view of the water lily pond hidden behind it, which you can hear but cannot see.

As the sound draws you further down the chipped bark path along the Japanese Garden, past tall grasses, an opening provides a view of the inviting hammock for two. Having a place to relax and enjoy each other's company was important to my client. Swaying in the hammock, she could experience the water lily pond in its full glory and also cool off in the afternoon shade from the tall trees nearby. The fountain in this pond directs the water flow in a circular pattern, filling all of the Wealth area with its radiating abundance.

Following the path back toward the house takes you by the Woodland Garden hidden in the shade under the large spruce trees in the Family gua. The compost bin is strategically hidden behind one large tree with daylilies planted in front. More daylilies and Kelly's rose bush (the burial place of a beloved pet) in the Knowledge area take you to a beautiful gate and a view of the front yard. Turning around and following the path back along the house, you pass a small Herb and Veggie Garden. This brings you to the flagstone patio and a view of the roses and birdbath next to the house, in Career. Water is the element for the Career area, and this water feature further enhances this area. A beautiful garden and a perfect solution to add more creativity and fun to a boring backyard.

HAMMOCK ROOM

Every garden should have a hammock, and using it as a focal point for an outdoor room is a perfect idea. After a difficult day at the office, or with the children, the weight of the world can feel heavy on your shoulders. In a hammock your body feels as light as a feather when you're gently swaying with the

Hammocks have a way of reminding us to take the time to enjoy ourselves in the garden

breeze. It relaxes you into a comfort mode of being securely held and cared for. The rocking motion is soothing and mothering to one's psyche. Usually when the hammock has been spotted in our yard, a mad dash is made to claim it for oneself.

I often sit in our double hammock with my daughter or son. We can look up into the tops of the majestic white pines and get a sense of how tall they truly are. Viewing the world from this horizontal perspective is one we often miss in our day-to-day lives. It brings back childhood memories of secret tree forts, or just lying back on a bed of freshly mown grass, watching the cloud parades float by.

I never really appreciated the fascinating upward growth of vine plants like virginia creeper, or even poison ivy, until viewed from this constantly moving perch. They are forever reaching, stretching to the sky. I love looking up at the green roadmap patterns on the undersides of their leaves.

My hammock is in the Family area of my garden. I placed it there intentionally to create an outdoor room for intimate conversations with my children. It is also where friends may join me, after a hot and sweaty day of gardening, or for an evening firefly show. There is something magical and childlike about a hammock. One gets giddy and playful trying not to be unexpectedly flipped into the dusty soil beneath it. There is a certain use of balance and partnership that occurs when it is shared. And alone it is the most peaceful and loving place to take a nap. I often bring a book to read, but it usually ends up on the ground rather quickly as I succumb to the hammock's hypnotic trance.

Hang yours in the shade if you want a cool place to relax after a long session of gardening in the summer. A sunny spot is ideal if you want to bask and soak up the sun on cool spring and fall days. I myself prefer one of each so that I have both options open, regardless of season or temperature.

SACRED PLANTS GARDEN

Setting aside a place to grow sacred plants in your garden can be an empowering experience. I am currently experimenting with white sage, sweet grass, cedar and tobacco. In the Native American tradition, these are the plants they call the four sacred medicines. These plants are used most often for ceremony and healing; used for carrying the prayers of their people and bringing them closer to the Creator.

I was under the impression that white sage would not grow in my planting zone five and survive the winter. Yet seeing it so plentiful on a mountaintop in Washington State, I thought I'd give it a try. The sage has made it through its first winter, which was a challenging one of below freezing and then thawing temperatures, and a weeklong severe ice storm as well. It not only survived, but is blooming and thriving! I'm hoping to re-seed this mother plant, and to purchase more now that the experimental year has passed. White sage is a mainstay for sacred space clearing work, as it energetically cleanses and lifts heavy vibrations in homes and for people. I also use it in my Medicine Wheel.

My sweet grass plant also does well in this garden. However confusing it with the lawn grass that so loves to invade this same area, I often inadvertently pull it up. I have discovered that it is true to its name and does taste sweet, so I'm often seen tasting a blade or two if I'm uncertain. Lawn grass is surprisingly very bitter in comparison.

Cedar grows by our vernal pond in the woods, and is considered a sacred tree, also used for smudging. A dream pillow filled with cedar is said to give one a restful nights sleep and pleasant dreams. There are many Native stories connected to the cedar tree; the following is one I often tell while sitting around the campfire, especially if there are cedars nearby.

CREATION STORY OF TURTLE ISLAND

A long time ago, there was a Spirit Being who walked the earth called the Wise and Gifted Being, the Strong Pure One, the Grandfather of Beings and Men; his name was Nanapush. During an unusually strong rainfall, he noticed that water began to rise rapidly, so he sought refuge and safety on the highest mountaintop. But the rain continued to fall, day in and day out, and the waters continued to rise, until there was only a small patch of ground on the top of the mountain. And on this patch of ground was growing a beautiful cedar tree. Its trunk was straight and tall, and it had many branches reaching out like straight arms in all directions.

The rain continued to come down, and soon it was apparent that all the seven continents, and all the mountains, would soon be completely covered with water. So the wise and great Nanapush picked up all the birds and animals that had gathered on the mountaintop with him, and tucked them safely inside his shirt. He then approached the cedar tree and spoke quietly to it, asking for its assistance before he started climbing. As he climbed, he broke off several branches and placed them under his belt.

When he reached the top of the tree he looked down and saw that the waters had continued to rise and were almost at his feet. So the great Nanapush began to sing and beat his drum, and the small tree began to grow, and it kept on growing straight and tall as the waters continued to rise beneath them.

After a time, Nanapush, the Strong Pure One, the Grandfather of Beings and Men, grew tired of singing his songs of peace to the raging elements, and threw his cedar braches into the water. They magically took the form of a strong and sturdy raft. Opon this raft the Great Being placed all the creatures he had saved, and they floated for some time upon this cedar raft. After several more days had passed, Nanapush decided it was time to create a new Earth; a task he could easily perform because of the powers the Creator had given him. And so he held a Council meeting with all the little creatures, and they began working together to form a new island.

Their first job was to get some soil from the now submerged Earth. The first to volunteer for this job was Loon. He was such a great diver, and stayed down for a very long time. Unfortunately, when he came to the surface he was exhausted, and did not have any of the soil with him. The next to offer to do the job was Otter. So Otter dove deep down into the water, yet also returned without any soil. The next to try was Beaver; surely he would be able to hold his breath long enough to do the task. But no, Beaver returned empty-handed also.

Then Nanapush turned to Muskrat and told him he must try very hard to reach some of the old Earth. Little Muskrat stayed down twice as long as any of the rest. When he came to the surface, completely exhausted but still alive, in his mouth and paws he carried some of the precious mud from the old world and Muskrat gave it to Nanapush. The great Nanapush was pleased; and he blessed the little Muskrat, promising that his kind would never die out.

Now Nanapush made a great ceremony, a Thanksgiving ceremony, the first Thanksgiving ceremony ever to take place. Then, Nanapush called for a helper who would receive and carry the new Earth. Turtle responded and was at once chosen to perform this important duty. Nanapush placed the mud brought back by Muskrat upon Turtle's back and blew his life-giving breath into it; immediately it began to grow. It grew and grew until it became the great island where all of us are living today. Because Turtle carried the new Earth on his back, this land upon which we live is called Turtle Island, the Place of the Great Turtle's Back.

Cedar is revered for it's strength, fast growth habit, and ability to grow tall and straight. It is also honored for it's sweet smelling branches when burned, but that is yet another story for another day.

GROWING TOBACCO

The Natives use sacred tobacco as a way of giving thanks in advance of receiving a gift from the earth. It is believed to carry the prayers of the people to the Creator. Well known for its use in the pipe ceremony, tobacco can also be gifted directly to the earth, to the water, and used in fire offerings. It brings with it a sense of comfort and oneness, although our common everyday use of tobacco is so addictive. Albert Sun Bear states, "I think God is trying to tell us something; taking that which is sacred, and to use profanely, may be hazardous to your health." Since using tobacco in offerings, I have grown a new respect for this powerful plant energy.

My search to find tobacco seeds has been fruitful. I will plant rose tobacco (*Nicotiana tobacum*), which has rosy trumpet shaped flowers and is said to be a beautiful ornamental plant, along with sacred tobacco (*Midewevian tobacum*), the native form of *Nicotiana rustica,* which is traditionally used in ceremony. I will dry it in the fall to include in my giveaway pouch for gifting the earth and it's plants.

Another traditional herbal/tobacco blend for giveaway, which can be used in the same way as tobacco, is Kinnikinnick. Kinnikinnick is a blend of herbs, tobacco, and bearberry (*Arctostaphylos uva-ursi*), a common plant found in northern forests of the United States. Bearberry's bright red berries stay attached to this low plant all winter long, providing survival food for bears when they emerge from hibernation; hence the name it is given. I collect it by the roadside on Drummond Island in Upper Michigan and use it to make a beautiful, energetic blend for honoring the plants. I place mine in a leather tobacco pouch, and refill as needed. The dried ingredients for this blend can be purchased at Mountain Rose Herbs listed on the product resource list.

✦ KINNIKINNICK TOBACCO OFFERING BLEND RECIPE ✦

MIX EQUAL PARTS:
bearberry and tobacco

ADD TO THIS MIXTURE:
red osier dogwood bark
yellow mullein leaves and flowers
sage
any other dried herb you feel called to add

MAKING A SAGE BUNDLE

Gathering white sage on a mountaintop in Washington State was a thrill for me. To experience this revered plant growing in its natural environment was a beautiful sight. As I picked this fragrant herb, I was awakened to memories

White sage bundle in an abalone shell holder

of Native American rituals and a sense of knowing I had done this many times before.

The best time to pick sage is in the early morning, after the sun has risen and the dew has evaporated from the leaves. Before picking sage from an individual plant, make an offering of tobacco, cornmeal, or Kinnikinnick, asking the Plant Deva's permission to do so. (If you are on private land, also get permission from the landowners.) Say a prayer and speak your intention for taking the parts of the plant. What do you intend to use it for? Let it know so that energy can be activated.

Cut the individual stems six to eight inches, or as long as the wand you wish to make. Gather together about five to six stems to make a bundle about two inches thick. Holding this bundle together tightly, take cotton embroidery thread of any color and tightly wrap it around the sage to hold the stems together. You can get fancy with patterns of diamonds by wrapping the thread in different directions, or you can simply wrap in one direction, spiraling upward. Tie off the end of the thread. Let the bundle hang for two to three days in a dry, shaded place. Enjoy the aroma! Saying prayers for its use is helpful during this drying time as you give thanks again to the plant for its giveaway.

INTERIOR GARDENS

During feng shui appointments in client's homes, I have noticed a distinct difference in the energy of a space that has green healthy plants as part of the decor. Notice I said healthy, for my teacher, Professor Thomas Lin Yun says, "No plant is better than a dead plant." I often gather blooming plants and floor plants together in one area of my home to create an indoor garden to help get me through the winter blahs. It is like my own miniature greenhouse. Positioning floor lamps with full spectrum light bulbs over the plants keeps them blooming and happy, as full sunny days in the winter are rare in Michigan. You can even add an indoor fountain on the floor, or on a stand, to give it a tropical feel and also to raise the humidity level. Lining the carpet with plastic and inexpensive tile creates a patio feel and helps protect floors from water damage.

I know the Plant Devas also come inside our homes, because I have seen their tiny pinpricks of golden light moving about these green spaces. The animals see them too: the cat usually stares and watches their movement and the dog just barks loudly.

These indoor gardens are a wonderful way to stimulate any area of the home's bagua. The Knowledge, Family, and Wealth guas would benefit most from this addition of so much wood element. Adding a water feature creates the nourishing cycle of water feeding wood, and wood feeding fire. Try placing several of these green islands throughout your home. Full spectrum bulbs can even replace regular bulbs in a table lamp that is close to your arrangement. This "natural sun" light is beneficial to the plants, and to you!

What is most important about indoor gardens or single plants is keeping them healthy. There is nothing worse visually and for Chi flow than seeing a half-dead, yellow, wilting plant in a corner, struggling to survive. If your plants look like this, please put them out of their misery and replace them. The added boost of Chi for your space will be well worth it, even if you have to replace them every six months!

Recently, I have attempted bringing in certain annuals to live during the winter in my home. Geraniums have faired the best, often blooming happily all season long. Impatiens work well as cuttings placed in decorative vases and re-planted in the spring. Herbs like bay leaf and rosemary stay in their pots year round, having outdoor summer vacations and coming inside before the first frost. Picking fresh basil for tomato sauce or rosemary for baked chicken helps to feed the misplaced gardener's Soul during the winter months. I even have palm trees that my son dug up in Florida that come inside with the cold weather. One day I envision them to be ten feet tall, standing in my living room and swaying in the breeze of the ceiling fan!

Wherever you live and whatever space you have can be used to create gardens with intention. Use you imagination to design an environment that you love to spend time in, and that nourishes your soul!

CHAPTER 9

CEREMONY IN THE GARDEN

Prayer is the activity of the invisible world,
yet its effect is actual and powerful.
It is said if you pray beside a flower it grows faster.
When you bring presence of prayer to the things you do,
you do them more beautifully . . .
to pray is to develop and refine the light of your life.
It smoothes the coarseness in your vision.
It brings you closer to the homeland of your heart.

John O'Donahue

SEASONAL GARDEN RITUALS

A spirit house purchased in Chiang Mai, Thailand and planted in the Spirit Garden

From Fall Equinox, to Winter Solstice, to the Spring Equinox and finally Summer Solstice, the year can be viewed as a series of opportunities for garden ceremonies that celebrate the seasons' movements. These sacred rituals in the garden are useful to remind us of our connection to the earth and its cycles.

Every third full month a new cycle of energy appears, yet the exact dates vary annually. It is best to consult a calendar for the date and time each year.

Know that the energies of the Solstices and Equinoxes, emerge up to three days before their exact date and times, and last up to three days after. It is very appropriate to do any of the following rituals during this extended time frame. The following ceremonies have been traditionally celebrated through the ages.

FALL EQUINOX OR MABON (*SEPTEMBER*)

Fall Equinox marks the starting point of these rituals for me. September may not coincide with the beginning of our calendar year; yet if you think about it, it does mark the beginning of Nature's cycle. This is when the magical seed is created, when all the life force energy of a plant is contained into one small and perfect unit. It is the initial birthing time of the essence of each particular seedling. Each of these individual packages of essence are just waiting for the right exterior conditions to grow. So autumn is the time to plant your new seed, to develop the essence of that which you wish to make manifest in the garden for the entire cycle of seasons to come. These are your seed thoughts, your visions, hopes, dreams, and aspirations for the future.

A favorite Fall Equinox or Mabon ritual, as it was called in Celtic times, is to gather the seeds of dried flowers and vegetables from your garden for next season. Penny Kelly, author of *The Elves of Lily Hill Farm,* says "the seeds which you produce from plants grown in your own garden, in your own soil, develop a cellular memory of how to grow in that particular environment". I can attest to this theory as my daughter's larkspur from her own gathered seeds are three times the size and vigor of larkspur I have grown from packaged seed in the same soil. It is as if they have learned how to adapt to these particular conditions. Place your gathered seeds in small envelopes or old film containers and label with name and date. Store in a dry, dark place. They will germinate best the first year, yet I have also had some seeds sprout that were two to three years old, just plant more if they are older.

Another fall activity is to harvest and dry medicinal herbs for teas to be used during the winter months. Speak to the plants before harvesting, explaining what your intention for using them will be. For example, I use the dried leaf of the wild raspberry to ease menstrual cramps and to nourish my body during moontime menses. I state this intention out loud while making an offering of tobacco, corn meal, or Kinnikinnick. With gratitude, I ask permission to use this plant for this purpose. I have found that herbs gathered in this honoring way make strong and powerful medicines.

WINTER SOLSTICE OR YULE (*DECEMBER*)

The next Nature holiday my family celebrates is Winter Solstice or Yule. We began to focus on this time of year because of the commercialization and craziness of Christmas. I often felt empty in December, wishing for something more, something different. The first year we officially celebrated this sacred week it reunited us as a family. During one of the busiest times of the year, we were meeting as a family every evening after dinner to prepare for our new holiday. The theme is always illumination and the return of the Sun. Living in cold (and often dreary) Michigan, this was a welcome idea!

We make homemade Solstice gifts for each other and friends, often involving some type of candle craft project. My favorite gift to make is decorating inexpensive, plain white candles with colored wax pens. Gold and silver spirals, stars, geometric designs, and even birds make beautiful candle art. Another year we hand dipped store-bought candles in melted beeswax. They looked and smelled heavenly!

In place of making the traditional Christmas cookies of reindeer and santas, we often make Solstice cutouts instead. Brightly colored suns, moons, and stars fill our cookie trays and link us to a remembering of Earth's intimate cycles.

There is a book called *Celebrating the Mother,* by Gail Johnson and Maura Shaw, which has become our family's resource for Earth celebrations. One Solstice activity inspired by this book is to create a Solstice Cave. I make a small cave-like structure in the garden or on the deck using stones and slate. In heavy snow years (when the rocks were buried), I have even used a large clay flowerpot on its side.

Family members then make small figurines for the cave. There is always a mother, a child, and an angel. The rest of the clay is then used for making

One example of a Solstice cave
made from rocks and slate

favorite totem animals, or other power symbols. (One year my husband made his red mustang convertible.) We have tried all different types of mediums; from salt dough, to oven clay, to air-drying clay, it has been fun to experiment. Because they are made new every year, it doesn't have to be permanent.

On Solstice Eve we place the figurines and animals in the cave, and lighting a small votive candle, saying prayers of gratitude for the Light in the darkness. We each speak a wish for the year ahead and then sing old carols like Deck the Halls or Good King Wenceslas. This singing is our way of joyfully ushering in the longer and brighter days ahead.

Our Solstice Cave is an ancient Celtic variation of the present day Christian nativity scene. In fact, visitors often mistake it for a traditional nativity scene when they see it; until they realize cougars, hawks, hummingbirds, and snakes surround the mother and child! Yet the mother symbolized here is not Mary but Mother Earth, and the child is not Jesus her son, but the Sun returning to us. In my own heart, these symbols *are* one and the same. Mary and the Earth both offering a nurturing and safe feeling of being deeply loved and always protected. The bright positive energy of Jesus doubles as the Sun in my life, expanding outward into all areas it touches. This ritual is a way I integrate my natural roots with my Christian belief in God in my present life.

Another winter Solstice Eve ritual we always do I've named *"Darkness in the House."* Children love this one, and often want to repeat it more than once. On Solstice Eve, before going outside to light the candle in the cave, we turn off all the lights in the house. Complete darkness is what is desired, so cover stove clocks, VCR lights, everything. Then, sit in the darkness together and experience what that feels like. Having become so reliant on electricity, we have forgotten that our ancestors used to live without it easily, not so long ago. Without lights, there is a quiet simplicity that fills the space, much like when the power goes out and our busy lives suddenly come to a standstill. Sit together and relish this darkness, relaxing into it and also noticing what, if any, fears come to the surface.

After some time, we put our coats and boots on and head to the Solstice Cave. It is now time to add the figurines and light the votive candle, experiencing that first flash of light that illuminates the darkness. Contemplate at this time what Light symbolizes for you. Is it clarity, is it ease of motion, is it the God source shining inside you?

After we have lit the cave, sung carols, and finished our rituals, we go back inside the house and light a single candle in each room. Make sure these candles are in safe votive holders and away from anything combustible. If you can find a safe place close to a window, that is ideal.

Once all the candles are safely lit, gather everyone together again and go outside, walking far away from the house until you can no longer see it. These evening walks in the dark woods or your own quiet neighborhood create magical memories. Pay attention to the moon and the stars. Notice any animals that may show themselves to you; they could be important signs for the coming year.

Now slowly walk back toward your home. When it first comes into view, seeing it lit with only the golden glow of soft candlelight is truly amazing. Stop and say a blessing on your home for the New Year and thank it for the shelter is has provided.

IMBOLC (*FEBRUARY 2*)

Imbolc represents the night when the Mother Crone of winter steps aside for the White Maiden Bridgid, who is pregnant with the Sun. Often bonfires or candles are lit on Bridgid's night to symbolize the heat or life force of the coming warmer season. Imbolc was renamed Candlemas by the Roman Christians, retaining this original fire symbology.

A ritual you can do on this night is to take any colored ribbon or silk scarf and leave it close to your doorstep after dark for Bridgid to bless. I sometimes tie mine to the doorknob, but I have also tied it around a favorite tree near the front of the house. Pray for Bridgid to take from you the things you do not wish to keep, and then ask for what you want her to help you find. Leave it outside overnight so she can bless it when she passes by your home. You can then sleep with this ribbon or scarf next to your pillow, or in your pillowcase, for the year ahead. You can also wear the scarf if you choose. This ritual is powerful for calling in transformation and healing.

SPRING EQUINOX OR OSTARA (*MARCH*)

The Spring Equinox is a time of great growth and joy. The waiting time of winter is over, and in the garden we are busy with soil preparation and filled with the desire to plant seeds. This festival, usually celebrated around the 21st of March, honors the time of year when day and night are equal in length. At Ostara, the earth finally begins to wake up, as the days grow longer.

We often blend our traditional Easter holiday with a Spring Equinox celebration. One obvious symbol for rebirth that is part of both traditions is the Easter egg. Making Easter eggs with natural dyes is a fun and educational project. Figuring out which foods will dye them what color is a lesson from our ancestors, who used natural dyes exclusively. Onionskins make a rich golden color, and beets or raspberries a beautiful rose shade. Blueberries make a pale blue dye, and spinach, kale, or parsley a wonderful light green.

Finely chop the materials until you have about one cup of each. Place each cup of product separately into two cups of water in a pan, and bring to a gentle boil. Reduce to a simmer for about 20 minutes, or until the water is

REAL GRASS EASTER BASKETS

I often like to actually "plant" Easter baskets with real grass. About two to three weeks before Easter, gather high handled baskets that have sturdy plastic liners. Fill with soil, plant heavily with grass seed, and water well. Place near a sunny window. Cover the top of the basket to retain warmth and humidity until seeds sprout. After sprouting, remove the plastic, water lightly, and mist often. You can do this in secret and surprise your children on Easter morning, or include them in this natural greening of their baskets.

well colored. Strain out the food material and add two tablespoons of vinegar to each cup of dye. Soak eggs in the dye until they are colored to the hue you desire.

One year, my son hand painted his with an edible brown paint, their spots matching the patterns and variety of natural birds' eggs. They looked beautiful in a homemade nest of moss.

Living on twelve acres of land has taken our Easter egg hunts to a whole new level. Often the adults will also participate in this game of hide and seek, and it is almost as much fun to hide the eggs deep in the woods as it is finding them. Those that are never found make surprise "gifts" for the raccoons and possums.

Homemade Incense

Because spring is related with the rising element of air, making homemade incense is another Equinox activity that honors this renewal of life force. There is something magical about grinding the dried herbs together and releasing their scent. One warm spring our family made incense outside on the deck, and then later that evening we had a fire in the outdoor fireplace. Watching the incense spark and ignite as it was thrown on the fire was great fun, and we also enjoyed the wonderful aroma.

Incense can also be used as a space-clearing tool in your home. A small bowl of natural incense placed in a room can quickly shift the mood and your experience of that space. Cinnamon is a scent most people enjoy, and conjures memories of the yummy taste of homemade cinnamon rolls. Lavender immediately brings on a sense of relaxation, and sage is often used for cleansing.

❧ INCENSE RECIPE ❧

3 parts broken up cinnamon sticks
2 parts dried lavender
½ part dried sage

Finely grind all ingredients together with a mortar and pestle. Use a small handful thrown on top of burning logs in a fireplace, or put some in a small container and place in desired rooms throughout your home. Crush or stir with your fingers to revitalize the scent. Lasts about 2 months.

Planting Quartz Crystal in the Garden

A Spring Equinox ritual that helps to prepare the gardens for their growing season is to plant quartz crystals there. Gather together natural quartz crystals of any size that appeals to you. Make sure they have been cleansed in sea salt or placed out in the sunlight for at least 24 hours. Proceed to plant these crystals into your gardens, speaking out loud your intentions of each area's growth for the upcoming season. You may place a single crystal per garden or one at each of its four corners; listen to your intuition and to the crystals, they will tell you where they need to go. After "planting" them, visualize in your mind the garden as flourishing and abundant, providing you with a bounty of vegetables or arms full of flowers. At this time you can also ask for the assistance of the Garden Devas or Nature Spirits of the land, and/or renew your commitment to working with them. Finish this ritual with a prayer of gratitude for the opportunity of being able to garden and connect with the incredible energy of the Earth.

BELTANE (*MAY 1ST*)

For many, May Day or Beltane holds a special forgotten memory in our hearts. It was celebrated in ancient cultures as a time to honor the fertility of the earth, and the bounty that it brings forth. A traditional May Day activity is, upon awakening, to go outside and bathe your face in the morning dew. It is said to bestow beauty all year long. My daughter and I do this every year, often when we are waiting at the early morning bus stop. Now you know our beauty secret!

A wonderful friend of mine, Leopoldine, shared her family May Day ritual with me. She lives in a small village high in the mountains of Switzerland. On the first day of May she wakes her four children up before the dawn, making sure they all dress in some green clothing. In perfect silence they go outside to wash their faces and also collect the morning dew into glasses. This water is used in sacred ceremony throughout the year. It is especially good for fertility rituals. Then they all walk to a favorite place high on a hill to watch the sunrise. As they see the suns golden light on the horizon, they sing this song, which I have loosely translated, to English:

Unite, Unite . . . and let us all unite
For summer has come today
And wherever we are going
We will all unite on this
Merry Merry morning of May.

If it is warm, they all go swimming in the river. Often they braid flower wreaths for their hair. Then they head back to their home, light all the candles inside, and do a spring space clearing of the energy in each room. The four elements are all represented during this clearing.

Leopoldine's May Day Space Clearing Ritual
Space clearing is a ritual to cleanse the stagnant energy of home, and to attract positive Chi flow into the space. She uses:

- ↪ Candles to represent Fire
- ↪ The collected dew to represent Water
- ↪ White sage bundle to represent Air
- ↪ Salt to represent Earth

Lighting all the candles placed in each room to activate the fire element, she then clears the energy in her home using the sage, water and salt. The dried sage bundle is lit and allowed to smoke as it is carried from room to room. With the children's help, the May water is sprinkled throughout each room and finally the salt is placed in the corners and the doorways to keep negative spirits away. After performing this annual ritual, the family appreciates the clean and fresh feeling created in their home for the year ahead.

SUMMER SOLSTICE OR LITHA (*JUNE*)

Summer is the final stage of the growing cycle. It is the true time of abundance for all we have been growing and nurturing. Growth in the garden is at an advanced rate; often Summer Solstice is a time when my garden is looking its best. There is an expansive energy present that brings all things to fulfillment, all the gifts and visual pleasures grown from those seeds and our plans that were made so long ago last fall.

Litha, or Summer Solstice, marks the longest day of the year when the sun's power is at its strongest. Ancient people, watching the sun reach its highest point at this time, often lit evening bonfires to encourage it to continue to shine and ripen their crops. This symbol of the bonfire teaches us that:

We, like the sun, have the power to nurture and sustain,
and that we have the responsibility to burn as brightly as we can.

Celebrating the Mother

Litha is still celebrated this way around the world. My husband's family belongs to a Finnish cultural group, which celebrates a special holiday they call Juahannus, at this same time of year. A large bonfire, or KoKo as they call it, is lit and all gather round and sing Finnish songs. This is their way of celebrating the halfway point of the year.

A fun solstice craft that boosts this idea of humans shining brightly like the fire or the sun is to make sun crowns. Anything placed on the head illuminates the crown chakra, or energy center, and makes a vivid connection between the sun's radiant energy and our physical body. Kings wore crowns to symbolize their connection to the heavens. One year, the children and I made our own crowns and all wore them during dinner. We felt like royalty! When making these head ornaments, the shinier they are the better. We used foil and glitter, yellow flowers and sun shapes. Metallic ribbon streamers can also be added.

We also decorated the house with sun-related art. One idea is to cut out a cardboard shape of the sun. Then cut a circle out of the center of this sun and fill this area in with yellow or orange tissue paper. These suns look beautiful hanging in windows, or from the ceiling where light shines through them, and can be left up all summer long if you like.

Gathering herbs from the garden for drying is also a traditional Summer Solstice activity. Wait until the morning dew has dried, then pick them and hang them upside down in a dry and cool place. Wild crafted herbs specifically gathered on this special day have a potent life force energy associated with them for medicinal use.

In Sweden, there is a traditional story that if you pick nine different flowers and put them under your pillow on the evening of Summer Solstice, you will dream at night about the one you will marry. Other countries have a tradition of leaving gifts for the Fairies on this night. They leave little cakes or biscuits in their designated fairy corner of the garden, or even a little tray of tiny things to eat, like cut up nuts and raisins, on dollhouse plates and tables placed there. In the morning, it is said, they would often find a small crystal in its place.

LABYRINTHS

Building and walking your own labyrinth is another ceremony appropriate for the garden. What is a labyrinth? A labyrinth is a path, usually circular in shape, which takes you on a singular journey. It is not a maze. There is only one way to the center, and to leave it, you must turn around and follow the same path out. I have read that some believe they can be portals for Nature Spirits to travel on from one place, or dimension, to another. I like to think the Spirits use mine to travel to the magical gardens in England all the time. Labyrinths are also quite helpful to use for walking meditation. Just begin at the entrance with a question clearly in your mind, and by the time you have traveled to the center and back an answer usually appears.

Ask a question on the way in, receive the answer by the way out

I was first introduced to the labyrinth at a weeklong workshop. It was a seven circuit one, meaning there are seven circular paths from the outer perimeter wall into the center. Painted onto a huge piece of canvas, it was a beautiful purple color with white paths. The teacher literally unfolded it outdoors onto the ground under some trees, and sacred space was created.

Friends and I came home from that class so inspired that we all decided we needed to have labyrinths to walk everyday. My friend Marjie took on the mammoth task of creating a flower and herb labyrinth, where the walls of the paths consist of perennials, herbs, veggies, and wildflowers. The paths are made of woodchips. It takes about an hour to walk through it because there is so much to see, touch, smell, and taste on the way. This is the perfect way to spend time in the present moment.

Another friend from class, who owned a fossil shop at the time, made hers out of blue flagstone on the side yard of a large lawn space, Each stone is about 12–14 inches in size, and between some she has placed beautiful chunks of amethyst, rose quartz, or a fossil or two. Hers winds through the grass on the lawn, and through some trees (it is delightful to play with their branches as you walk by), with everything buried low enough so that she can still run a mower over the area. (Being extra careful around the special stones of course.) She also has two large hunks of rose quartz at the entrance, and a few rare and special stones placed at the center.

I came home from the workshop and wanted an even quicker, easier labyrinth fix; so my son and I mowed one in the grass field in front of our home. The mowed grass, as wide as the mower is, became the path. It is simple to maintain, as you just mow it when it gets scraggly.

I also helped a friend with the placement of a wheel-chair-accessible labyrinth at the Nature Education Center near the local high school. Choosing where to build it was a fun experience, as we spoke with the Nature Spirits quite regularly. After a few visits, it was clearly decided, with their assistance, where the labyrinth was to be placed.

Another friend has used a path of antique paving bricks buried level with the grass for her labyrinth, with a Buddha statue placed in the center, which she walks and takes offerings to every day. Research has show walking a labyrinth helps to balance the right and left hemispheres of the brain. I know it helps to keep me centered and more fully present in the moment.

MEDICINE WHEELS

Medicine Wheels are sacred symbols used to represent the vast knowledge of the universe. Several years ago, I was drawn to build my first Medicine Wheel on the property where we lived then. I chose a very special oak tree, growing in the middle of a red pine forest, for its center. Every year, near the time of Fall Equinox, a fairy ring of large white mushrooms would appear around this tree. Learning from author, Ted Andrews, that fairy rings can also be doorways or portholes to other dimensions, I decided this was the perfect place for my sacred site.

BUILDING A MEDICINE WHEEL

It was with great reverence and ceremony that I created my first Medicine Wheel. I began by trance walking to collect five stones, four inch or so in diameter, and five natural sticks, two to three feet in length. I learned the simple, yet powerful, act of trance walking from Denise Linn – just walk with your eyes partially closed and your mind focused on what you are looking for. As I walked along carrying a large tote bag, I asked to be shown the rock and stick that were to mark the East, the South, the West, the North, and the Center of my wheel.

Stakes used to make the four directions being honored on the Medicine Wheel altar

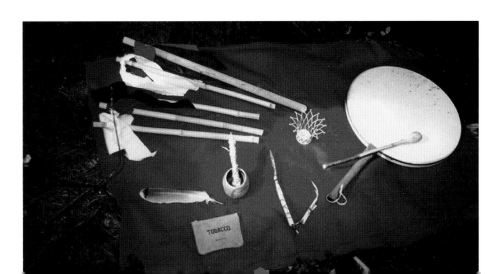

With the sticks, I made ceremonial flags by tying colored strips of cotton fabric onto them. The colors I used for these directional markers were: yellow for the East; red for the South; black for the West; white for the North; and blue/green for the Center. These colors are derived from one Lakota interpretation of the Medicine Wheel; be aware that colors used to symbolize each direction often vary, even among the same native group. Use what colors "feel" right to you.

After smudging everything with white sage, including myself, I began to place the stones and flags. Starting with the East, I placed the East rock with the yellow flag, saying my prayers to that direction and calling its energy into the Wheel. From there I moved directly to the Center of the wheel, which was the tree, and at its base placed the center rock and blue/green flag. The Center space in this Wheel represents Mother Earth, and I said my prayers to her, thanking her for supporting me and helping to anchor and hold the energy form I was creating. Moving from Center, I walked to the South direction and anchored that rock and the red flag, saying prayers and asking for the energies of the South to enter the Wheel. From there I headed back to the center, honoring the Mother again before moving to anchor the West arm of my wheel with the rock and black flag. Walking back to the Center, I prayed again, and proceeded to the North to place the white flag and North rock, finishing in the Center of the wheel. Then I walked slowly around the inside perimeter of the wheel, offering cornmeal trailing from my fingers to connect this circle, joining together all of the energies I had just invited to create a truly sacred space.

This Wheel fills me with a sense of deep spirituality, a closeness with God that I have not found anywhere else. Often I have tried other places of worship, but find myself sitting in the pew daydreaming of being in my Medicine Wheel instead. For me, it is a sanctuary where I go to pray, ask questions, and just feel close to Creator. I use this Wheel for outdoor meditations by myself and with students, and for drumming circles. It is also the place I hold rituals, especially during Solstice and Equinox. Experiencing a full moon, glimmering across the white snow on Solstice Eve, is one of my favorite memories.

From the beginning, I decided before entering the Wheel, I would always smudge myself and any articles I brought into the space. This makes my intentions for using the Wheel stronger and also helps me to slow down, contemplate, and keep the space sacred.

While in this Native American Lakota-based Wheel, I often meditated on how, or even if, I could blend it with the feng shui bagua. It has always been my desire to incorporate these two traditions into the work that I do. Meditating on this, I was told both are boundaries for creating sacred space, and both represent the cycles of life; yet each is unique in and of itself, to be used separately.

My experiences meditating inside the fairy ring at that Medicine Wheel were amazing. This was during a time in my life when I was growing more open to the presence of the Nature Spirits in my garden, and had just begun working with them. They would often appear to me there; again as tiny pin pricks of light in the air all around my head, and began to share with me a lot of the information you have been reading in this book.

Since that time I have moved to another home and moved the energy of that first Wheel to where I am located now. Before removing the colored stakes and rocks, I ceremoniously gathered up the energy of the Wheel up in my minds eye, and intentionally sent it to the new property, traveling easily on a rainbow bridge of light. I asked it to please wait there for me – until I was able to locate and place the new Medicine Wheel structure. Then, with much prayer and gratitude for how it had served me, I slowly dismantled the physical symbols of my wheel, giving the stones back to the earth and burning the flags and stakes in a ritual fire.

Below find directional information I have received while meditating in the Wheel. While providing a helpful overview, the best way to get to know the directions personally is to spend time facing each direction and sense what guidance they can offer you.

The prayers I use to honor the four directions in the Wheel are also included. With an offering of cornmeal, tobacco, sage, or incense face the direction and speak from your heart. Always start in the East when entering the Medicine Wheel.

EAST

The color I use for the East is yellow like the rising sun, the sacred plant connected to it cedar. East is the entrance point on the wheel. This is the place of the dawn and the morning star, the direction of the spring and new beginnings, the place of youth. When you have a question about where or when to begin a project, or are facing something new in your life, seek answers in the East. This is the place of creation, of "endless possibilities."

EAST PRAYER: *I call to the direction of the East to be in my circle today. I ask that the energy of Air be with me, and guide me to the clarity and wisdom I desire. The East is the place of new beginnings, and as I begin this journey, and this day, I ask for your support through the air I breathe and the wind that surrounds me. Aho*

SOUTH

The color I use to represent the South is red. The plant honored here is tobacco.

This is the place of high energy, the spirit of summer. This is where you cultivate your passion in life. A time of gaining knowledge, gathering information for your ideas, filling yourself up to the brim. Use the energy of the south to generate emotion and enthusiasm in your life as you manifest your creative ideas.

SOUTH PRAYER: *I call to the direction of the South to be in my circle today. I ask that the energy of Water come to me and cleanse me with its refreshing qualities. I know the South is the place of my emotions, of my fears and my passions. Please guide me to listen to these messages from my Soul, who speaks through my emotions, that I may hear and understand all that flows through me. Aho*

WEST

Black is the color associated with the West direction. The sacred plant I use here is sage. This is the place of death and rebirth; the direction you face to seek the Truth. Here we refine down to the bare essence all the information we have gathered. This is the season of Indian Summer and Fall. Spend time here to go within and reflect on that which you have learned, and let go of any burdens you no longer need.

WEST PRAYER: *I call to the direction of the West to be in my circle today. I ask that the energy of Fire be with me to reveal my shadow side like a candle shining light into the darkness. The West is the place of transformations, of death and rebirth. May I be rebirthed into my new self, and all that was once hidden, please gently be revealed to me now. Aho*

NORTH

The color I use to represent the North in my wheel is white. The sacred plant for this direction is sweet grass. This is the place of wisdom. Found here are the Wise Beings, and this is the direction in which to seek counsel from them. A true knowingness is found here; not that of just *doing,* but of *being.* It is the place of our elders and guardians, the quiet season of winter wrapped in a blanket of snow. It is a place of deep peace.

NORTH PRAYER: *I call to the direction of the North to be with me in my circle today. I ask that the qualities of Earth be near, to guide and ground me on my life path. The North is the place of the Wise Ones and my ancestors. May I feel your loving presence in my life and hear the wisdom that you speak. Aho*

NORTH BACK TO EAST

This area completes the circle. This is the place of the afterlife, where you go when you die. It is a place of remembering – remembering *who* you are on a Soul level, remembering your true immortality – as you follow the path of the circle, before being rebirthed into the East again.

CENTER

The colors of blue and green are placed in the Center of my Wheel to represent Mother Earth and Father Sky. The sacred plant I use in this space is

Kinnikinnick. Stand here in the center of the circle and symbolically also stand in the center of your life. Feel the pull of Mother Earth at your feet, grounding your spirit to her. Feel the nurturing effect that gravity has on your physical being. Safe, sturdy, and protected, feel the energies of the four directions all around you. Now become aware of your connection to the heavens above. Father Sky, Grandmother Moon and Grandfather Sun. Feel the Oneness, of we are each such a small yet essential part of. Feel the Great Spirit of us all!

CENTER PRAYER: *As I stand in the Center of my circle today, may I feel the nurturing of dear Mother Earth beneath my feet. May I always remember our connection to one another in this life experience. May I see and feel Father Sky and the vast stars of the universe above my head. May I always be reminded of the protective canopy you provide. With immense gratitude for all that I receive every day, I say thank you! Aho*

EXPERIENCES IN THE WHEEL

There have been many sacred and enlightening experiences that have happened in the Medicine Wheel. Here are two of my favorites.

Moontime Ceremony

When my daughter was twelve years old she experienced her first menstrual cycle, or moontime as we call it. It was important to me that we marked this special occasion. We had been discussing plans for a celebration for a few years now, and my joy and enthusiasm for this rite of passage had not spilled over into her idea of what this day would mean. I had originally wanted to throw her a big party with all of her girlfriends, envisioning starting a new trend among the other families that they might do the same for their daughters. Soon realizing this was not what she wanted, we compromised on dinner out with the family following a private ritual in the Medicine Wheel with just the two of us.

Planning this rite required me to meditate first on what would be most empowering for her at that time. She was nervous, and a bit scared of this idea of "growing up," yet part of her wanted to embrace it with confident open arms. As I sat in meditation, the faces of all of her grandmothers and great-grandmothers came into my vision. I also saw Marianne Williamson's book, *Illuminata: Thoughts, Prayers, Rites of Passage,* and knew there would be some important words to find there.

So on a warm afternoon in October, we solemnly headed out to the Medicine Wheel. I could tell Jessica was unsure of what we would experience, yet she also seemed inwardly pleased to be doing ritual with her Mom.

Outside the entrance to the Wheel we lit a sage stick, sitting in its beautiful abalone shell, and with a feather drew the smoke over each other's body for purification. She then followed as I walked the perimeter of the wheel, slowly releasing corn meal and tobacco from our fingers, and ending back at the East where we had started.

Entering the wheel, after leaving another offering of a piece of our hair wrapped around the East flag, we headed to the center to set up an altar. On a large piece of red wool as the foundation, we placed silk colored scarves in her favorite colors of deep green and sea blue, along with framed photos I had gathered of her grandmothers and great-grandmothers. We also unpacked three sets of divination cards. Our drums were removed from their carry bags and placed to the side. I lit a small votive candle and we were ready to begin.

Standing together, starting with the East, I spoke out loud prayers to the four directions, asking for their assistance for Jessica specifically from each of these unique energies.

I then talked about her ancestors, the incredible women in the photos placed before us. They had come to me in meditation to be included, as a part of the linage of women my daughter had now also joined. Their DNA was in her blood, as well as their strength and fortitude. Some photos, like the one of her grandmother as a young and sexy girl, she had never seen. Others showed her great-grandmothers and great-great-grandmothers whom she never met, and she wanted to know more about them. After telling their personal stories,

I let her know that all of these strong women were always available to guide her, whether physically alive or not. It felt appropriate to be honoring this important linage in both of our lives, and I could strongly sense their presence in the Medicine Wheel that day.

Setting this stage of support, we then read the ritual words I had adapted from Williamson's beautiful book, *Illuminata*. I have included my adaptation below. You can easily use these words for your daughter(s); just fill in the information at the underlined places. With a few changes, these ceremonial words could also be adapted for marking a son's rite of passage.

My daughter then picked her cards from each of the divination decks, and we talked about what they might mean for her at this time. She picked *Transformation* from one set, which stated, "A big change in your life is at hand, you are at the beginning of an enormous transformation in your life." The affirmation following this explanation made her smile, as she read out loud, "I am joyously centered and safe as wonderful changes occur around me!" We then just talked, mother to daughter, on that beautiful fall day; with her asking me a lot of questions about moontime, such as "It happens every month for 5–7 days?" and how she was going to integrate this into her life now.

We closed with a drumming circle, and she felt honored to be using my most sacred frame drum. Her visions were around what she wanted this moontime to mean to her; and mine were more bittersweet, as I quietly cried with tears of gratitude at seeing all the precious cycles of womanhood that lay before her. It was all so beautiful, and a great afternoon in the woods together with my daughter. The Medicine Wheel had served us well, providing a sacred place to perform this important ceremony. We than gathered all of our belongings, and exited the Wheel walking backward out the East doorway, saying our prayers of gratitude as we left.

Vision Quest

A Vision Quest is a Native American ritual used to intentionally quiet the mind and go within to hear wisdom from the Soul. It is often experienced in Nature in a designated sacred space, such as a Medicine Wheel.

PUBERTY RITE OF PASSAGE RITUAL

[Ceremony leader]
We are gathered here together to celebrate the entrance into womanhood of
NAME OF HONOREE, *this beautiful child of the Creator.*

NAME OF HONOREE, *on this day you are asked to enter formally with me into the adult population of the world. You have lived for ____ years; and have come to the final stages of your childhood. Although I cannot offer you a perfect world, I invite you now to participate with me in the sacred task of healing it and making it whole.*

From this day forward, with mine and your family's blessings and support, may you be open to the call of your destiny. Know you are the full director, along with Creator, of its movement through your life.

[Honoree responds]
I sit openly before you, having lived over ____ years on this Earth. Now, in full consciousness, I dedicate the rest of my life to the Creator in all and to my purposes here on Earth. I am an (personal ethnic identification) and draw strength from the legacy of those who came before me. I honor you, my family and loved ones, for what you have done and not done to make the world I inherit a place of love and peace.

[Ceremony leader]
NAME OF HONOREE, *with this ceremony you enter into the community of adulthood. May you know in your life the joys of full and abundant womanhood. May the world honor you for who you are. Wherever you go, our love and blessings go with you.*

AMEN

There was a time in my life when I felt pulled in several directions at once. Having started to seriously write this book, I was also running a business and teaching classes; I wanted to sort out where to best focus my energy. I decided to go on a Vision Quest.

When I awoke that morning it was snowing and about 30 degrees outside. Knowing I could be in the wheel for several hours, I decided to wait until afternoon with possible warmer temperatures. At 2:00 PM it was still freezing out so I decided to change plans and create a sacred circle in my office instead. Entering my office with every intention of having the Vision Quest there, a loud voice inside my head said, "Get outside you wimp! This ceremony and you need to be *outside* and in your Medicine Wheel now!" So I gathered all the supplies needed, again the voice telling me what to bring (even adding some extra blankets and warm socks)!

Heading down the path through the pines to the Wheel, it felt as if something was moving my body other than me. Every step I took was surreal, as if propelled by another force. With drum and bags and wool blankets over my shoulder, visions of being a Native in another time came into my mind.

Outside the Wheel, I smudged everything being brought into this sacred space, including myself. Leaving an offering of tobacco and sage, I then entered at the East flag. I smudged the complete inside edge of the circle with sage, and then followed with a cornmeal offering. Heading to the Center to set up the altar, I laid out a smaller circle of items on my blanket of red wool to honor the four directions. In the East, to represent the Air element, was placed the still smoldering smudge pot, and several feathers. They were a large goose feather, a beautiful swan feather, and an awesome tiny dove wand. In the South was placed a small clear bowl of water with a few colorful river stones in the bottom. In the West was a small candle in a beautiful, yet safe, dish, to represent the Fire element. For the North, a golden piece of citrine represented the Earth. At the Center a beautiful double terminated quartz crystal amplified this prayer beneath it.

We are one global family,
all colors, all races, one world united.
We dance for peace and the healing of our planet Earth.
Peace for all nations.
Peace for all communities.
Peace within ourselves.
Let us connect heart to heart.
Through our diversity we recognize our unity.
Through our compassion we recognize peace.
Our love is the power to transform the world.
Let us send it out . . .
Now!

After standing and saying prayers, and making cornmeal offering to all of the directions, my Vision Quest began. Sitting in a comfortable position, with my back supported by a tree, I relished and relaxed into the peacefulness surrounding me. The woods felt wonderful on this cold afternoon, and I was warmed from a glow within. I drummed, hummed ancient tunes, and focused on NOTHING for over an hour. My external awareness went to the wind, watching as it played with the smudge smoke, twirling and flowing, so much like Chi that *it was Chi*.

As I drummed, the crows joined me with their calls. One large bird flew overhead calling; the rest were hidden in the trees somewhere. I was very pleased by this messenger, as crows represent magic and the spiritual side of life to me. It was then that I asked the question, "If I knew my spiritual path right now, what would it be?" I was told quite clearly, "to be the Mother, to write your book, and to garden. The rest are just obstacles you have placed in your path. They are excuses you use to keep from following you heart's desire." Yes, when focused on those three topics, my heart sings and I smile. They are what I am here to do.

After receiving this meaningful vision, the second half of my time was used on heartfelt prayers. I have never prayed so hard and so deeply for so many people at one time before! It made me realize how many wonderful people are in my life to pray for, and tears of gratitude came gushing forth. I spoke out loud the prayer for the world that I had placed in the Center under the large crystal; and it was empowering to see the words magnified through the stone. Closing with some drumming, I noticed the birds, squirrels, and other critters in the forest sensing the rhythm along with me as it echoed through the woods. Their accompaniment helped me to feel so connected with everything there. This Medicine Wheel experience opened my eyes to remembering I am here to feel my bliss. I learned from this time to say "Yes" to all opportunities that deal with being a Mom, writing my book, or connecting with the garden. I learned it was okay and perfectly right to say "No" to all that would take me in the opposite direction. It all became so clear, the Quest fully revealed.

GREEN TRIBUTES

The best time to plant a tree was 25 years ago. The second best time is now.

Unknown

I love the idea of planting a tree to mark a moment in time. A good friend planted a Red Maple to commemorate the birth of her first child. They went to the nursery when he was just a few months old and together picked it out. She said Micah reached out his sweet little hand and grabbed this particular tree and smiled. It was clearly the one to bring home. They planted the Maple and watched it grow year by year. When Micah was four years old they chose to move to Texas, yet because they still have family and friends here, they visit often. And, driving by their old house and seeing the Micah tree growing by leaps and bounds, just like its namesake, still remains a thrill for them.

I also know a woman who planted a tree in front of her first home to commemorate a sad miscarriage that she had experienced while living there. Twenty years later, after having moved completely out of the state, she attended a weeklong Spiritual Retreat that was held at a college right down the street from her first home. Taking a walk, she went back to visit her previous home and there in the front yard stood that very same tree. It had grown sturdy and tall, just like the child would have grown had it lived. Though the memories were difficult to face, she said some heartfelt prayers and collected fallen branches and seeds from this tree to take home with her. This revisiting of the past, twenty years later, helped heal an emotionally wounded part of her that she had carried for so long.

There are also heirloom plants passed down from family generations that remind us of the depth and continuation of life. These are plants that can be traced back to several generations of family care. I have the most beautiful yellow aromatic daylily that was from my favorite Aunt Mil's garden. Hers was the first magical garden I was introduced to as a child. It had vine-covered

This fragrant yellow daylily, a family heirloom plant, has been passed down through the generations

gates and winding pathways that led to unknown places in my imagination. It was full of singing birds you could see and hear from the bathroom window in the morning if you stopped to watch. I have memories of seeing the sunlight shining on the sweet smelling baby pink rose trellis and the orange spotted tiger lilies nodding in the breeze. She and my mother could spend hours in her garden talking, digging, and transplanting their favorite flowers. I vowed, then and there, I would have a garden like that someday; a garden one would love to get lost in.

This particular yellow lily represents all that and more to me, and has been moved and divided many times. My first plant was a house-warming gift from my mom, who of course received her first transplanted lily many years before from Aunt Mil. The known family tree of this particular lily plant can be traced all the way back to my great-grandmother's garden in Indiana. It has since traveled to all of my Michigan homes, leaving a trail of heavenly scent and gorgeous yellow flowers in its wake. I'm sure it will continue its journey to my grown children's gardens one day, and perhaps even to some nieces and nephews homes!

When my son was three years old, we created lilac memories I know neither of us will ever forget. Living in the city at the time, our home had several large lilac bushes growing at the side of the garage. It was just a nondescript green bush eleven months out of the year; but in May, it was in its glory! With hundreds of sweetly scented white and light lavender conical blooms, Stephan and I clipped to our hearts content. I can still see his face surrounded by these beautiful lilac blossoms as his arms overflowed with this amazing bounty. Soon the dining room table was covered with newspapers and piled high with flowers, while we gathered every empty vase in the house. With Mom clipping, and son happily given the job of pounding the stems on a cutting board with the hammer, we arranged flowers for every room in the house. The smell of lilacs in the Spring always takes me back to that magical day, and I know it does for Stephan too!

Jessica and I also have a sweet Nature connection with a lush pile of soft green moss. While walking down our two-track driveway to school every day

The fragrance and beauty of lilac blossoms make wonderful childhood garden memories

when she was very young, we once discovered a mound of moss that looked amazingly similar to a profile of a small furry bunny, ears and all. Sitting on its haunches, it grew at the base of a large pine tree; and each spring, a group of naturalized purple-blue grape hyacinths sprouted nearby. Admiring the grape hyacinths is what really drew us to find the *Bunny Moss* in the first place. I can still see Jessie as a kindergartener, in her fancy dresses, bending over this "bunny" and petting it and talking to it every day to and from her way to the bus. I swear the more we talked to it and called it the *Bunny Moss*, the more it began to hold the shape of an actual bunny!

So now it is time to go and create your own stories of magical gardens and heirloom plants. It is time to look at your garden or natural spaces with new eyes. Eyes that can see how the ancient art of placement can be applied to your gardens, to literally "see" the flowing Chi of life surrounding you.

You can begin by just taking a simple walk in Nature, but this time take it *with* Nature. Spending some quiet meditative time in the woods, or in your garden, can be the start of opening doorways to full conversations with the Nature Spirits found there. Make an herbal concoction with your own hands, even if it is just a simple mint tea. Pay attention to the rhythms found in Nature, and cycle with her by planning your own personal ritual, even if it is just looking for the full moon every month.

Does your mother, your grandmother, a dear older friend or neighbor garden? Ask them the history of some of their favorite plants. Find out if there is a special heirloom plant that has been passed down from generations, and ask for a division from it to keep this legacy and its Nature connection alive for years to come.

It is never too late to deepen, or even to start, a relationship with the green and growing world. There is so much to be gained by cultivating a true reverence for our Earth and the gifts she provides us. It can be as easy as stepping out your own back door.

Animal Deva – Deva in charge of a particular animal family/species.

Bagua – eight-sided map used over designated spaces to determine the placement of the nine life conditions of feng shui.

Ceremony – movements and prayers used with intention to bring about a desired result.

Garden Deva – the energetic life force responsible for the growth of all living things in a specific garden space.

Fairy – energetic life force found in an individual flower or plant in charge of producing flowers, fruits, and leaves of that plant.

Feng Shui – the study and art of placement within environments in order to enhance the life force available to that space.

Giveaway – a sincere offering given with intention for a service provided.

Infusion – mixing plant material with liquid to extract its medicinal and energetic qualities.

Labyrinth – a circular path used to create a balance of the right and left hemispheres of the brain.

Medicine Wheel – a circular sacred space used to represent our life path and our place in the universe.

Mouth of Chi – entrance on the bagua map where the largest amount of life force energy enters a determined space.

Nature – God's energy made manifest here on Earth.

Nature Spirit or Deva – a condensing of Nature energy through the four elements of air, water, fire, and earth.

Overlighting Deva – Nature Spirit or Deva in charge of all life force that is present for a particular area, animal species, insect species, or element.

Plant Deva – Deva in charge of a particular plant family/species.

Ritual – movements and prayers preformed by rote memory for a specific intention.

Tincture – infusion of plant material, water, and natural preservative to be used as medicine.

↔ BIBLIOGRAPHY

Andrews, Ted. *Animal Speak*. Minnesota: Llewellyn, 1993.

———. *Animal Wise*. Tennessee: Dragonhawk Publishing, 1999.

Balter, Gaylah. *Gardening With Soul*. Arizona: The Learning Tree, 2003.

Bear, Sun Wind, Wabun, and Mulligan, Crysalis. *Dancing with the Wheel*. New York: Fireside, 1992.

Cole, Rebecca. *Potted Gardens: A Fresh Approach to Container Gardening*. New York: Random House, 1997.

———. *Paradise Found: Gardening in Unlikely Places*. New York: Random House, 2000.

Collins, Terah Katheryn. *The Western Guide to Feng Shui*. California: The Crossing Press, 1998.

Cowan, Eliot. *Plant Spirit Medicine: The Healing Power of Plants*. North Carolina: Blue Water Publishing, 1995.

Gladstar, Rosemary. *Herbal Healing for Women*. New York: Simon and Schuster Inc., 1993.

Hamilton, Geoff. *The Organic Garden Book*. New York: DK Publishing, 1993.

Harper, Peter. *The Natural Garden Book*. New York: Simon and Schuster Inc., 1994.

Hodson, Geoffrey, *Fairies at Work and at Play*. England: Theosophical Publishing House, 1987.

Hoffman, David. *The New Holistic Herbal*. Great Britain: Element Books Limited, 1990.

Hyder, Carol J. *Wind and Water*. California: The Crossing Press, 1998.

Johnson, Cait, and Shaw, Maura. *Celebrating the Great Mother*. Vermont: Destiny Books, 1995.

Kelly, Penny. *From Soil to Stomach*. Michigan: Lily Hill Publishing, 2005.

———. *The Elves of Lily Hill Farm*. Minnesota: Llewellyn, 1997.

Linn, Denise. *Feng Shui For The Soul.* California: Hay House, Inc., 2000.

———. *Sacred Space.* New York: Ballantine Books, 1995.

———. *Soul Coaching Cards.* California: Hay House Inc., 2005.

Lonegren, Sid. *Labyrinths.* New York: Sterling Publishing Co. Inc., 2001.

Olkowski, W., Doar, S. *Common Sense Pest Control.* Conn.: Taunton Press, 1991.

Rossbach, Sarah, and Prof. Lin Yun. *Living Color.* New York: Kodansha International, 1994.

Steiner, Rudolph. *Nature Spirits.* England: Rudolph Steiner Press, 1995.

Tompkins, Peter, and Bird, Christopher. *The Secret Life of Plants.* New York: Harper and Row Publishers, 1973.

Wardwell, Joyce. *The Herbal Home Remedy Book.* Vermont: Storey Publishing, 1998.

Williamson, Marianne. *Illuminata.* New York: Random House, 1994.

Wright, Machaelle Small. *Behaving as if The God in all Life Mattered.* Virginia: Perelandra Ltd., 1987.

———. *Perelandra Garden Workbook.* Virginia: Perelandra Ltd., 1987.

 PHOTO ACKNOWLEDGEMENTS

A gray tree frog, named 'Cutie Pie',
honoring a hanging fuchsia plant

When someone gives you a gift from the heart, expecting nothing in return, that is a true gift. So many friends and family members have contributed to the beauty of this book with their photographs, and I am grateful their loving energy has become a part of *Spirit Gardens*. Photo acknowledgements in order of appearance:

Susan Haifleigh – cover, page i
Karen Jarldane – pages ii, xii, 124, 134
Deb Swingholm – pages 9, 20, 80, 103, 114
Dani Plazanet – page 14
Neshi Lokotz – pages xvi, 23, 43
Mimi Ray – page 25
Donna Thompson – page 27
Tracy – page 28
B.J. Gorman – page 54

Sandy Mudra – page 68
Stephan Kansman – pages ii, 93, 185
Oliver Vanpe – page 97
Cindy Garreton – page 106
Dani and Tina Ehlenfeldt – page 156
Leslie Morrison – author photo page 192
Minnie Kansman – pages ii, v, vi, xvi, 4, 31, 34, 42, 57, 60, 63, 67, 70, 77, 82, 91, 105, 112, 117, 129, 131, 139, 147, 153, 160, 169, 171, 183, 190

PRODUCT RESOURCE LIST

Bach flower remedies
Bach flower essence tincture
www.bachflower.com

Beneficial insects
Lacewings, trichogramma wasps, ladybird beetles
www.gardensalive.com
www.beneficialinsectco.com
Praying mantid egg cases
www.beneficialinsectco.com

Dried herbs, tincture bottles, and containers
Mountain Rose Herbs
www.mountainroseherbs.com

Feng shui round faceted crystals
Crystal Cove
www.starry-eyed.com/prisma/gallery/home.hmtl

Native American frame drums
Neshi Lakotz
www.two-feathers.org

Soil test kits
Accugrow Soil Test Kit
www.GardensAlive.com

Tobacco Seeds
Tobacco seeds from around the world
www.seedman.com

White sage bundles
Victoria White Eagle
www.victoriawhiteeagle.com

ABOUT THE AUTHOR

Minnie Kansman began her feng shui consultation business Eco-Balance Humanity in Harmony with Nature in 1994. She is a graduate of Commercial Floriculture from Michigan State University, and has worked in the floral design business for over 15 years. She now concentrates her energy as a Master Feng Shui Consultant, Feng Shui Garden Consultant, and Soul Coach. Residing in a log home in the Michigan woods with her husband, children, and Samoyed puppy Leo, she lives lightly on the land, honoring all of Nature's gifts.

If you would like to experience a private home or phone consultation, host a garden lecture or workshop in your city, or learn more about Minnie's upcoming classes, please visit her at her website

www.minniekansman.com